Critical Challenges for Primary Students
(Revised Edition)

An interdisciplinary collection of critical thinking lessons for students in the primary grades

Authors

Tami McDiarmid

Rita Manzo

Trish Musselle

Editors

Maureen McDermid

Roland Case

Series Editors

Roland Case

LeRoi Daniels

TC^2

The Critical
Thinking Consortium

Series published by

The Critical Thinking Consortium
University of British Columbia
Education Building
6365 Biological Sciences Road
Vancouver, BC Canada V6T 1Z4
Tel: 604.822.9297
Fax: 604.822.6603
E-mail: tc2@interchange.ubc.ca
www.tc2.ca

Series distributed by

Pacific Educational Press
Faculty of Education
University of British Columbia
Vancouver, BC V6T 1Z4
Tel: 604.822.5385
Fax: 604.822.6603
www.pep.educ.ubc.ca

McGraw-Hill Ryerson, School Division
300 Water Street
Whitby, ON L1N 9B6
Tel: 905.430.5247
Fax: 905.430.5023
www.mcgrawhill.ca

Cover Design: Antonia Banyard
Interior Design: M. Kathie Wraight, Field Programs, Simon Fraser University
Production: M. Kathie Wraight, Field Programs, Simon Fraser University
Cover Photograph: Primary students from Vivek High School, Chandigarh, India

The Critical Thinking Consortium is especially grateful to the **Vancouver Foundation** for its financial support of this resource and many of the other volumes in this series.

First edition, 1996

Second edition, 2007

Library and Archives Canada Cataloguing in Publication

McDiarmid, Tami, 1960-
    Critical challenges for primary students : an interdisciplinary
collection of critical thinking lessons for students in the primary
grades / authors, Tami McDiarmid, Rita Manzo, Trish Musselle ; editors,
Maureen McDermid, Roland Case. -- Rev. ed.

(Critical challenges across the curriculum series, ISSN 1205-9730)
ISBN 978-0-86491-284-8

    1. Critical thinking--Study and teaching (Primary) I. Manzo, Rita, 1955-
II. Musselle, Trish, 1968- III. Critical Thinking Consortium. IV. Title. V. Series.

LB1590.3.M36 2007   372.13   C2007-905268-1

Introduction

Critical Challenges

Table of Contents

Critical Challenges Across the Curriculum is an ongoing series of teacher resources focussed on infusing critical thinking into every school subject. Two features distinguish this series from many other publications supporting critical thinking—our *curriculum embedded* approach and our emphasis on *teaching the intellectual tools.*

Our approach is to embed critical thinking by presenting focussed questions or challenges that invite critical student reflection about the content of the curriculum. We do not see critical thinking as a generic set of skills or processes that can be developed independently of content and context. Nor do we believe that critical thinking can adequately be addressed as an add-on to the curriculum. Rather, if it is to take a central place in the classroom, critical thinking must be seen as a way of teaching the content of the curriculum. Teachers can help students understand the subject matter, as opposed to merely recalling it, by providing continuing opportunities for thoughtful analysis of issues or problems that are central to the subject matter.

The second distinguishing feature of this series is its emphasis on systematically teaching a full range of tools for critical thinking. Much of the frustration teachers experience when inviting students to think critically stems from students' lack of the required concepts, attitudes, knowledge, criteria, or strategies—in short, they lack the tools needed to do a competent job. It is often assumed that the mere provision of invitations to think will improve students' reflective competence. We believe that constructing a thoughtful response is like building a house in that it is impossible to do a competent job in either case without the necessary tools. For this reason, every critical challenge in the series includes a list of the tools needed to respond competently and, more importantly, activities suggesting how these tools may be taught and assessed.

We hope primary teachers will find these resources of use in increasing and improving the teaching of critical thinking with their students.

Roland Case & LeRoi Daniels
Series Editors

Foreword

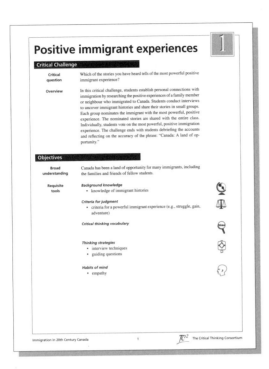

Each **critical challenge** opens with a **question** or **task** which is the focal activity upon which the lesson is based. An **overview** describes the topic and the main activities that students undertake.

Broad understanding is the intended curricular understanding that will emerge as students work through the challenge.

Requisite tools provides an inventory of specific intellectual resources that students need to competently address the critical challenge:

Background knowledge — the information about the topic required for thoughtful reflection;

Criteria for judgment — the considerations or grounds for deciding which of the alternatives is the most sensible or appropriate;

Critical thinking vocabulary — the concepts and distinctions that help to think critically about the topic;

Thinking strategies — procedures, organizers, models or algorithms that help in thinking through the challenge;

Habits of mind — the values and attitudes of a careful and conscientious thinker that are especially relevant to the critical challenge.

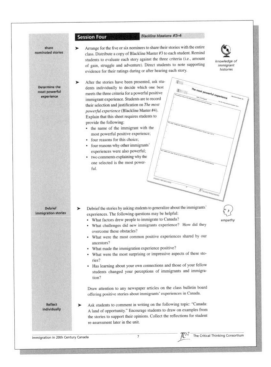

The body of the lesson is found under **suggested activities** that indicate how the critical challenge may be introduced and how the requisite tools may be taught.

Where relevant, **sessions** indicate where each anticipated new lesson would begin and the blackline masters needed for that session.

Down the left-hand panel is a handy **summary of main tasks** or activities for each session.

Icons along the right-hand side point out where specific tools are addressed.

Also provided in **evaluation** are assessment criteria and procedures, and in **extension** are found suggestions for further exploration or broader application of key ideas.

References cited in the suggested activities or recommended for additional information are often listed.

Blackline masters *are found immediately after individual lessons or, in the case of a sequenced unit, at the back of the volume. These are the reproducible learning resources referred to in the suggested activities. They serve a wide range of purposes:*

- **assessment rubrics** *identify suggested criteria and standards for evaluating student work;*

- **briefing sheets** *provide background information for students;*

- **data charts** *contain various organizers for recording and analyzing information;*

- **documents** *refer to primary source material, including paintings and other illustrations;*

- **student activities** *provide questions and tasks for students to complete;*

- **transparencies** *refer to material that can be converted to a transparency for use on an overhead projector.*

Electronic sourcebook *is a web-based supplement to our print publications. These materials include colour reproductions of pictures, primary documents, and updated links to other sites.*

- *If electronic resources had been developed at the time of publication, the available resources are referenced in the Suggested Activities.*

- *Periodically we update or supplement the print volumes with additional electronic information and resources.*

To locate referenced materials or to see whether new material has been developed, access our website and look for the title of this publication under the Electronic Sourcebook *heading.*

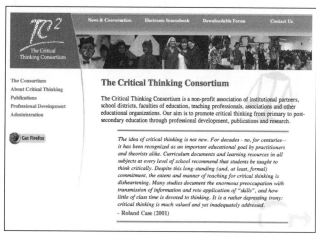

For more information about our model of critical thinking consult our website — www.tc2.ca

Understanding critical thinking

Critical thinking involves thinking through problematic situations about what to believe or how to act where the thinker makes reasoned judgments that embody the qualities of a competent thinker.

A person is attempting to think critically when she thoughtfully seeks to assess what would be sensible or reasonable to believe or do in a given situation. The need to reach reasoned judgments may arise in countless kinds of problematic situations such as trying to understand a passage in a text, trying to improve an artistic performance, making effective use of a piece of equipment, or deciding how to act in a delicate social situation. What makes these situations problematic is that there is some doubt as to the most appropriate option.

Critical thinking is sometimes contrasted with problem solving, decision making, analysis and inquiry. We see these latter terms for rational deliberation as occasions for critical thinking. In all these situations, we need to think critically about the available options. There is limited value in reaching solutions or making choices that are not sensible or reasonable. Thus, the term critical thinking draws attention to the quality of thinking required to pose and solve problems competently, reach sound decisions, analyze issues, plan and conduct thoughtful inquiries and so on. In other words, thinking critically is a way of carrying out these thinking tasks just as being careful is a way of walking down the stairs. Thus, thinking critically is not a unique *type* of thinking that is different from other types of thinking; rather, it refers to the *quality* of thinking. The association of critical thinking with being negative or judgmental is misleading, since the reference to critical is to distinguish it from uncritical thinking—thinking that accepts conclusions at face value without any assessment of their merits or bases. It is more fruitful to interpret critical in the sense of critique—looking at the merits and shortcomings of alternatives in order to arrive at a reasoned judgment.

Our focus on the quality of thinking does not imply that students must arrive at a preconceived right answer; rather, we look to see that their varied responses exhibit the qualities that characterize good thinking in a given situation. For example, it wouldn't matter whether students opposed or supported a position expressed in a newspaper or textbook. Regardless of their particular position, we would want students' critically thoughtful responses to exhibit sensitivity to any bias, consideration of alternative points of view, attention to the clarity of key concepts and assessment of supporting evidence. We believe that emphasis on qualities that student responses should exhibit focusses teachers' attention on the crucial dimension in promoting and assessing students' competence in thinking critically. The challenge for teachers is to adopt practices that will effectively promote these qualities in their students.

Promoting critical thinking

To help students improve as critical thinkers, we propose a four-pronged approach:

- build a *community of thinkers* within the school and classroom;
- infuse opportunities for critical thinking—what we call *critical challenges*—throughout the curriculum;
- develop the *intellectual tools* that will enable students to become competent critical thinkers;
- on a continuing basis, *assess students' competence* in using the intellectual tools to think through critical challenges.

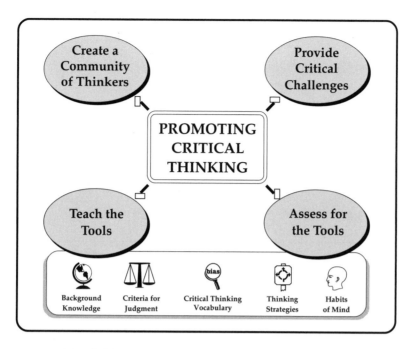

Building a community of thinkers

Developing supportive school and classroom communities where reflective inquiry is valued may be the most important factor in nurturing critical thinking. Many of the intellectual resources, the "tools" of critical thinking, will not be mastered by students unless their use is reinforced on an ongoing basis. As well, the image of the thinker as a solitary figure is misleading. No one person can perfectly embody all the desired attributes—we must learn to rely on others to complement our own thoughts. There are many routines and norms that teachers can adopt to create a community of thinkers:

- Regularly pose questions and assignments requiring students to think through, and not merely recall, what is being learned.

- Creating ongoing opportunities to engage in critical and cooperative dialogue—confer, inquire, debate and critique—is key to creating a community of thinkers.

- Employ self- and peer-evaluation as ways of involving students in thinking critically about their own work.

- Model good critical thinking practices. Students are more likely to learn to act in desired ways if they see teachers making every effort to be open-minded, to seek clarification where needed, to avoid reaching conclusions based on inadequate evidence and so on.

Infusing critical challenges throughout the curriculum

If students are to improve their ability to think critically, they must have numerous opportunities to engage with and think through problematic situations—what we refer to as *critical challenges*.

- *Does the question or task require judgment?* A question or task is a critical challenge only if it invites students to assess the reasonableness of plausible options or alternative conclusions. In short, it must require more than retrieval of information, rote application of a strategy, uninformed guessing or mere assertion of a preference.

- *Will the challenge be meaningful to students?* Trivial, decontextualized mental exercises often alienate or bore students. It is important to frame challenges that are likely to engage students in tackling questions and tasks that they will find meaningful.

- *Does the challenge address key aspects of the subject matter?* Critical thinking should not be divorced from the rest of the curriculum. Students are more likely to learn the content of the curriculum if they are invited to think critically about issues embedded in the subject matter.
- *Do students have the tools or can they reasonably acquire the tools needed to competently address the challenge?* Students need support in acquiring the essential tools required to competently meet the critical challenge.

Developing intellectual tools for thinking critically

The key to helping students develop as critical thinkers is to nurture competent use of five types of tools of thinking. These categories of tools are *background knowledge, criteria for judgment, critical thinking vocabulary, thinking strategies* and *habits of mind.*

Background Knowledge
—*the information about a topic required for thoughtful reflection*

Students cannot think deeply about a topic if they know little about it. Two questions to ask in developing this tool:
- What background information do students need for them to make a well-informed judgment on the matter before them?
- How can students be assisted in acquiring this information in a meaningful matter?

Criteria for Judgment
—*the considerations or grounds for deciding which of the alternatives is the most sensible or appropriate*

Critical thinking is essentially a matter of judging which alternative is sensible or reasonable. Students need help in thinking carefully about the criteria to use when judging various alternatives:
- Is my estimate *accurate*?
- Is the interpretation *plausible*?
- Is the conclusion *fair* to all?
- Is my proposal *feasible*?

Critical Thinking Vocabulary
—*the range of concepts and distinctions that are helpful when thinking critically*

Students require the vocabulary or concepts that permit them to make important distinctions among the different issues and thinking tasks facing them. These include the following:
- inference and direct observation;
- generalization and overgeneralization;
- premise and conclusion;
- bias and point of view.

Thinking Strategies
—*the repertoire of heuristics, organizing devices, models and algorithms that may be useful when thinking through a critical thinking problem*

Although critical thinking is never simply a matter of following certain procedures or steps, numerous strategies are useful for guiding one's performance when thinking critically:
- *Making decisions:* Are there models or procedures to guide students through the factors they should consider (e.g., a framework for issue analysis or problem solving)?
- *Organizing information:* Would a graphic organizer (e.g., webbing diagrams, Venn diagrams, "pro and con" charts) be useful in representing what a student knows about the issue?
- *Role taking:* Before deciding on an action that affects others, should students put themselves in the others' positions and imagine their feelings?

Habits of Mind
—*the values and attitudes of a careful and conscientious thinker*

Being able to apply criteria and use strategies is of little value unless students also have the habits of mind of a thoughtful person. These include being:
- *Open-minded:* Are students willing to consider evidence opposing their view and to revise their view if the evidence warrants it?
- *Fair-minded:* Are students willing to give impartial consideration to alternative points of view and not simply to impose their preference?
- *Independent-minded:* Are students willing to stand up for their firmly-held beliefs?
- *Inquiring or "critical" attitude:* Are students inclined to question the clarity of and support for claims and to seek justified beliefs and values?

Assessing for the tools

Assessment is an important complement to teaching the tools of critical thinking. As suggested by the familiar adages "What is counted counts" and "Testing drives the curriculum," evaluation has important implications for what students consider important and ultimately what students learn. Evaluations that focus exclusively on recall of information or never consider habits of mind fail to assess, and possibly discourage, student growth in critical reflection.

A key challenge in assessing critical thinking is deciding what to look for in a student's answer. If there is no single correct response, we may well ask: "On what basis, then, can we reliably assess students?" In the case of critical thinking, we would want to see how well students exhibited the qualities of a competent thinker. Thus, the intellectual resources or tools for critical thinking become the criteria for assessing students' work. The following example suggests specific assessment criteria for each of the five types of critical thinking tools that might be considered when evaluating critical thinking in an argumentative essay and an artistic work.

Type of criteria for assessment	Evidence of critical thinking in a persuasive essay	Evidence of critical thinking in an artistic work
Background Knowledge *Has the student provided adequate and accurate information?*	• cited accurate information.	• revealed knowledge of the mechanics of the medium.
Criteria for Judgment *Has the student satisfied relevant criteria for judgment?*	• provided ample evidence; • arranged arguments in logical sequence.	• was imaginative; • was clear and forceful.
Critical Thinking Vocabulary *Has the student revealed understanding of important vocabulary?*	• correctly distinguished "arguments" from "counter-arguments."	• represented "point of view."
Thinking Strategies *Has the student made effective use of appropriate thinking strategies?*	• used appropriate strategies for persuasive writing.	• employed suitable rehearsal/preparation strategies.
Habits of Mind *Has the student demonstrated the desired habits of mind?*	• demonstrated an openness to alternative perspectives; • refrained from forming firm opinions where the evidence was inconclusive.	• was open to constructive criticism; • demonstrated a commitment to high quality; • demonstrated a willingness to take risks with the medium.

Overviews of Critical Challenges

As many primary teachers have known for years, young children can think for themselves and think critically provided they are given appropriate conditions and directions. The 18 challenges in this collection illustrate how to teach the tools that will empower primary students to think critically qbout various topics across a range of subject areas.

Community/environment

 Building structures

3 sessions

Students learn about basic principles of construction and about using criteria to judge performance. Students build assigned structures that satisfy specific criteria set by the teacher. They are also asked to explain why their structures may meet or fail to meet each of the criteria. As an extension, students generate their own criteria and attempt to build a structure that satisfies these requirements.

 Photo caption

3 sessions

In this two-part challenge, students are asked to take a photograph that depicts a previously chosen feature or quality of their community (e.g., friendly, dangerous, fun). Other students try to match the quality with the photograph and explain why the photograph reflects this quality.

 Design a community

3 sessions

After extensive study of communities, students brainstorm the qualities to be found in a good community and the services and facilities that best provide for these qualities. Students then design an ideal community using materials of their choice. Students explain how the desired qualities are reflected in the facilities and services in their plan.

 Insect habitat

3 sessions

In this two-part challenge, students observe various insects in the classroom or the natural environment, and study them in films and books. Students work together to identify the features of a desirable insect habitat. Students use these criteria to design a habitat for an insect of their choice. Throughout these activities, students are encouraged to ask informative questions about the life of insects.

 Problem in a picture

3 sessions

Based on a picture card from the *Second Step* series, students explore a situation depicted in a photograph involving a child feeling unwelcome. After brainstorming possible solutions, students select and give reasons for the best solution based on criteria they have generated. Students are encouraged to see that problems can be addressed in several ways but that some solutions are better than others.

Human nature

 The wolf's "real" character

3 sessions

Students consider a traditional version of the "The Three Little Pigs" and then examine *The True Story of the Three Little Pigs* by Jon Scieszka. In the non-traditional version, the wolf claims to have been unfairly characterized as the bad guy. Students are encouraged to find evidence in the text to support their own conclusion about the wolf's real character. They are asked to see through the obvious rationalization offered by the wolf.

 Predicting a winner

2 sessions

In this challenge, students consider whether or not the author in *The Boxing Champion* by Roch Carrier is likely to win his boxing match. Part-way through the story, students use clues in the text to predict the outcome and justify their prediction. Because the author paints an unrealistic portrait of his prospects, students must infer why he may not win his bout.

 It's so nice to have a wolf around the house

2 sessions

In this challenge, students consider whether the wolf, Cuthbert Q. Devine in *It's So Nice to Have a Wolf Around the House*, is a hero or a scoundrel. Students are asked to look for evidence for both conclusions and to be open to the possibility that things may not be as they first appear. After sharing the evidence students have found, they are invited to reconsider their initial conclusion about Cuthbert.

Moral dilemmas

I **The discovery**

3 sessions

In the story *Jack and the Meanstalk* by Brian and Rebecca Wildsmith, Professor Jack discovers a way of dramatically increasing the size of plants. Students brainstorm the possible consequences of this discovery and weigh the pros and cons before deciding whether or not Professor Jack's secret should be shared with the rest of the world.

Rumpel-stilstkin and the conditions for kindness
3 sessions

In this challenge, students consider when it is that they have a responsibility to help others in need and when they do not. They then view the film *Rumpelstiltskin* and listen to the story before deciding whether Rumpelstiltskin was right to demand something from the miller's daughter in exchange for saving her life.

 Making a difference

3 sessions

In this challenge, students consider what they can do to make a lasting difference in someone else's life. The inspiration for the challenge is the picture book *A Handful of Seeds,* by Monica Hughes, which tells of a girl in Latin America who helps a group of street kids. Students identify criteria for selecting an action that they might do to make a lasting contribution to others' well-being. They review possible actions in light of these criteria, and in groups of three select and explain their proposal for making a difference.

 Right to do wrong?

3 sessions

In this two-part challenge, the stealing of a trumpet in E.B. White's novel, *The Trumpet of the Swan*, is used to focus discussion on when, if ever, it is justifiable to do something that is wrong. In the story, the parent of a young swan steals a trumpet to provide the young voiceless swan with a way to communicate. Other stories raise a similar dilemma—*Robin Hood* (stealing from the rich to give to the poor) and *Jack and the Beanstalk* (stealing a hen to provide food). Students are asked to offer their preliminary opinions about the acceptability of the swan's action and the appropriateness, in unusual situations, of doing something "wrong." They then explore the impact of the action on each of the characters in the story before reassessing their initial opinions.

Me and my family

 My character traits

4 sessions

In this challenge, students explore the positive features that others in the class would associate with them. Students begin by considering that some people may have an unrealistic picture of themselves. They distinguish character or personality traits that are positive from those that are negative or mixed. Using this knowledge, students choose three positive traits that reflect how others see them. Other students then try to guess which students are described by the identified traits.

 Powerful positive memories

3 sessions

In this challenge, students are introduced to the concept of memory though the story, *Wilfred Gordon McDonald Partridge* by Mem Fox. This story of an elderly woman who is aided in regaining her lost memory by a little boy is used to stimulate students into thinking about the range of memories they have. After recalling a number of them, students individually select a most powerful positive memory, and explain what makes it so significant.

 Assigning household tasks

4 sessions

In this challenge, students are asked to assign household tasks to members of their family. *Piggybook*, by Anthony Browne, is used to introduce the idea of sharing household chores in a fair manner to the class. Students identify four important tasks in their homes, and decide how they might fairly and safely allocate them to family members.

 The trouble with Mama

3 sessions

In this challenge, students explore the qualities a good parent has. The story, *Monster Mama*, tells of a typical seven-year old whose mother is a Monster. After considering what makes a good parent, students locate four pieces of evidence from the story to help them reach a conclusion about Monster Mama.

Learning from others

 **Powerful questions**

3 sessions

In preparation for a visit by a classroom guest or written interviews of community members, students identify criteria for a "powerful" question. In groups, students brainstorm possible questions and then use the criteria to critique questions they have generated. Each student selects a powerful question to ask the designated respondent.

The value of money

3 sessions

In this challenge, students choose an activity that will enable other students to demonstrate their mastery of a specified outcome involving money. Students examine the curricular learning outcomes related to money, and brainstorm possible activities that would involve one of these outcomes. They then discuss the criteria for a good demonstration task and select an activity that best reflects these criteria.

Building structures

Critical Challenge

Critical task   Build a structure that meets the specified criteria.

Overview   Students learn about basic principles of construction and about using criteria to judge performance. Students build assigned structures that satisfy specific criteria set by the teacher. They are also asked to explain why their structures may meet or fail to meet each of the criteria. As an extension, students generate their own criteria and attempt to build a structure sthat satisfies these requirements.

Objectives

Broad understanding   Structures can be created through careful trial and error that meet specifications.

Requisite tools

Background knowledge
- basic principles of construction

Criteria for judgment
- specified criteria for the structure (e.g., rigidity, strength, stability)

Critical thinking vocabulary
- hypothesis and hypothesis testing
- criteria

Thinking strategies

Habits of mind
- attention to detail

The Critical Thinking Consortium

Suggested Activities

principles of construction

Pre-planning

➤ Assemble a set of the following construction materials for each pair of students:

- toothpicks (50)
- plasticine (approximately 1/2)
- heavy manila tag (for reinforcement).

Session One   *Blackline Master #1*

Explore construction materials

➤ Allow students time to explore and play in pairs with the plasticine and toothpicks. Meet to discuss with pairs of students what they discovered about the properties of those materials:

- What were you able to do with the materials?
- What was the plasticine useful for?
- What were the toothpicks useful for?
- Did you make a strong shape?"

Make a simple construction

➤ Ask students to make use of what they found out about the materials, to construct either a box-like shape or a rigid pyramid (i.e., does not wobble). Ask one half of the class to construct a box (or cube) and the other half to construct a pyramid. Allow students sufficient time to work and investigate, then call them back into a large group and discuss their findings.

Introduce and use criteria for construction

➤ Explain to students that the two conditions—a particular shape (either a pyramid or a box) and a specific design feature (no wobble)—are referred to as "criteria." Explain that criteria are features we use for judging whether we have been successful at our task.

Provide pairs of students with *Checking our structure* (Blackline Master #1) on ledger-sized paper. Together, decide and record whether or not their structures met the criteria. (May be enlarged.)

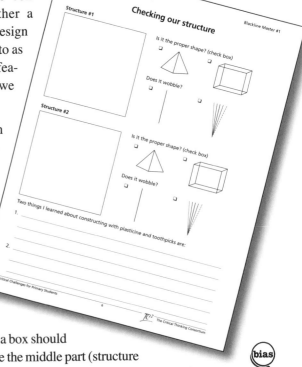

Assign new shapes to construct

➤ Invite students to make a rigid, strong shape. Students who initially made the pyramid should try to make the box. Students who initially created a box should make a pyramid. Ask students to use the middle part (structure #2) of Blackline Master #1 to judge their new structure. Discuss their findings with the whole class.

bias

criteria

Indicate lessons learned

➤ With older students, invite them to answer the sentence seen at the bottom of Blackline Master #1—Two things I learned about constructing with plasticine and toothpicks are:

criteria for the structure

1. _____

2. _____

Session Two   *Blackline Master #2*

Establish criteria

➤ Present the challenge by explaining to students that the next structure they build must meet three criteria:

- must be a specific *height*   7 centimetres

- must support a given *weight*   200 grams

- must be constructed *within a materials allowance*   using fewer than 50 toothpicks, fewer than 10 manilla tags, and placticine in separate lumps that are no larger than the size of green peas

Provide tools to measure requirements

➤ To help students determine if their structure meets these criteria, provide each pair with the following:

- ruler (for measuring height)

- small book or other weight of about 200 grams (to be used to test supporting weight)

- green pea (to judge size of plasticine).

Create and test structure

➤ Allow students sufficient time to create their structures, and encourage them to pay close attention to whether or not they have met the three criteria.

With older students, provide each pair of students with a copy of *Generating and testing hypotheses* (Blackline Master #2).

attention to detail

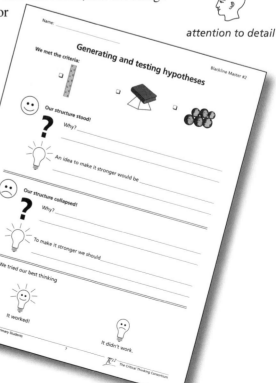

➤ If their structures collapse, ask students to generate a hypothesis to explain why, and then test their hypothesis to see whether it makes their structure stronger. If their initial structure successfully supports the weight, ask students to generate a hypothesis explaining why it did so.

*hypothesis and
hypothesis testing*

Session Three

➤ Invite students to share their structures and hypotheses with the whole class. With younger students, invite pairs to share their structures, collapsed or intact, and suggest reasons for the result. Encourage them to suggest how to build a stronger structure and list their ideas on a chart for future constructions. Such a list might be a good addition to a kindergarten construction centre where students could try to generate and test their hypotheses.

Evaluation   *Blackline Master #3*

➤ Assess students' understanding of how to use criteria to judge a construction using the first criterion on *Assessing student constructions* (Blackline Master #3). The sources of evidence for making this assessment are listed below:

- Use responses of the working pairs in the class discussion of initial constructions, on *Checking criteria* (Blackline Master #1), to assess their ability to use the identified criteria to judge the stability of their construction and to apply their learning to their subsequent constructions.

- Use responses on section one of *Generating and testing hypotheses* (Blackline Master #2) to judge students' ability to meet the specific criteria for the task.

➤ Assess students' understanding of hypothesis generation and testing using the second criterion on *Assessing student constructions* (Blackline Master #3) to judge their ability to analyze, hypothesize and test. The sources of evidence and criteria for making this assessment are listed below:

- Use individual responses in class discussion and/or responses by pairs on *Generating and testing hypotheses* (Blackline Master #2) to assess their ability to analyze their structure and suggest reasons for success or suggestions for re-construction.

- Use results of pair testing and explanations to the whole group to judge students' ability to design and carry out a test of their hypothesis.

Reaching the "basic understanding" level on the rubric may be appropriate for early primary students.

Extension

Read a story

➤ Follow up the lesson by reading the story *Tar Beach*, by Faith Ringgold.

Create student-designed challenges

➤ Ask students to create their own challenges using the same materials by setting different criteria for height, weight and materials allowance (e.g., How many supplies do they think that they might need?). Invite students to consider how they will test the structure's strength, height, and whether it was within the required materials allowance.

Reference

Tar Beach by Faith Ringgold (New York: Crown Publishers, 1991).

Checking our structure

Structure #1

Is it the proper shape? (check box)

❑   ❑

Does it wobble?

❑   ❑

Structure #2

Is it the proper shape? (check box)

❑   ❑

Does it wobble?

❑   ❑

Two things I learned about constructing with plasticine and toothpicks are:

1. _____

_____

_____

2. _____

_____

_____

Generating and testing hypotheses

We met the criteria:

❑ 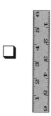   ❑    ❑

  Our structure stood!

     Why? _____

_____

     An idea to make it stronger would be _____

_____

  Our structure collapsed!

     Why? _____

_____

   To make it stronger we should_____

_____

Testing: We tried our best thinking

It worked!   It didn't work.

Assessing student constructions

	Sophisticated understanding	Extended understanding	Basic understanding	Partial recognition	Pre-recognition
Uses criteria to judge/revise structures	Uses the criteria to design and assess the success of the structure and to make additional improvements.	Uses the criteria to assist in building the structure and may be able to use one or two to assess the success of their structure.	Understands the criteria and can use them, with assistance, in building the structure.	Understands what is asked, but does not use the criteria in building the structure.	Does not understand what it means to use criteria to build a structure.
Generates and tests hypotheses	Generates one or more plausible hypotheses for the success or failure of the structure and designs and completes tests.	Can generate a plausible hypothesis and suggest and attempt a possible test.	Can generate a simple hypothesis for the success or failure of the structure.	Makes suggestions about the success or failure of the structure that may not be accurate or reasonable.	Cannot suggest a reason for the success or failure of the structure.

Comments:

Photo caption

Critical Challenge

Critical tasks
A. Select the photograph that best shows the quality of the community that you have been assigned.

B. Match a photograph with the most appropriate caption.

Overview
In this two-part challenge, students are asked to take a photograph that depicts a previously chosen feature or quality of their community (e.g., friendly, dangerous, fun). Other students try to match the quality with the photograph and explain why the photograph reflects this quality.

Objectives

Broad understanding
The qualities of a community can be recognized in everyday scenes.

Requisite tools

Background knowledge
- knowledge of a community
- how to use a camera

Criteria for judgment
- features of a good photograph (e.g., fits a caption, has sufficient detail)
- criteria for an appropriate match (e.g., caption fits evidence in the photograph)

Critical thinking vocabulary
- evidence, reasons

Thinking strategies

Habits of mind

$\mathcal{TC}^2$ The Critical Thinking Consortium

Suggested Activities

Pre-planning

Obtain cameras

➤ Secure enough cameras so that there is one for each group of four students. Cameras that produce an immediate image are preferable for this activitiy (i.e., digital, polaroid).

Build prior knowledge

➤ To complete these challenges students should be familiar with the qualities that characterize a successful community.

Session One   *Blackline Master #1*

Brainstorm community descriptions

➤ Ask students to brainstorm words (adjectives) that describe their community environment (e.g., friendly, happy, fun, dirty). Write each word (or phrase) on a separate index card and place the cards in a large envelope. These words are now captions. Students in pairs choose a card from the envelope without looking. Each pair of students keeps the card (with caption) they picked to themselves.

knowledge of community

Explain the task

➤ Explain to students that they will go out into the school grounds (or the neighbouring community) with a partner to take three photographs that show the quality indicated on their index card. Encourage students to take different angles of the same scene, or take photographs of different scenes.

Discuss criteria for good photographs

➤ Before sending students out, discuss the criteria of a good picture. This may be done by sharing several photographs of varying quality that you have taken to represent a particular quality (e.g., a happy family). Ask students to identify notable features about each photograph. Three criteria are particularly key for this activity:

features of good photographs

- the image is large enough to be recognizable

- there are sufficient details to send a message

- the image matches the caption.

➤ If desired, show students a set of three photographs of varying quality that represent a common feature (e.g., a sad family). Using *Selecting a good photograph* (Blackline Master #1) as a guide, rate how well each photograph meets the specified criteria. Discuss which photograph best shows the identified quality.

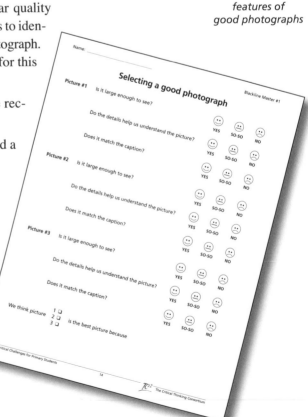

**Explain use
of cameras**

➤ If students are unfamiliar with the use of cameras, provide instructions and a few tips for taking good photographs. Cameras that produce photographs immediately are most appropriate for this activity.

use of a camera

Session Two

**Give students their
photo assignments**

➤ Working in groups, ask students to take three photographs within the school grounds (or in the neighbouring community) that capture the particular quality of the community they have been assigned.

**Introduce the
first critical task**

➤ When students have returned to the class with their photographs, introduce the first critical task to the class:

> *Select the photograph that best shows the quality of the community that you have been assigned.*

Review the criteria for a good photograph and help each pair of students use Blackline Master #1 to rate the three photographs on each of the criteria before selecting the best one to represent the assigned caption.

**Post photographs
and captions**

➤ When each pair of has selected its best photograph, tape all the captions on one part of the board and all the photographs on another part.

**Present the
second critical task**

➤ Present the second critical task to the class:

> *Match a photograph with the most appropriate caption.*

Each pair takes a turn pointing to their picture (without revealing which is their caption) while other members of the class guess which caption belongs with the picture and explain why they think it fits.

**Match pictures
and descriptors**

➤ Allow the class three guesses for each picture. If a guess is correct or after three failed guesses, the pair explains to the class what caption their picture represents and gives their reason for taking this picture to represent their caption.

Check for understanding

Play a matching game

Provide reasons for choice

➤ Use either of the following activities to check for understanding by inviting students to match pictures to captions and explain reasons for their choice(s).

With younger students, place the captions in a pocket chart or attach to a board. Play a matching game by inviting students to choose one or more photographs that they think matches the captions. Ask them to place the photograph next to the caption and give reasons for their choice. This may be done in pairs or individually.

With older students, provide each student with a copy of *Matching captions* (Blackline Master #2) and invite them to choose a caption, find the best picture from those available and write the reasons for their choice. Multiple copies of pictures can be photocopied if necessary for this activity.

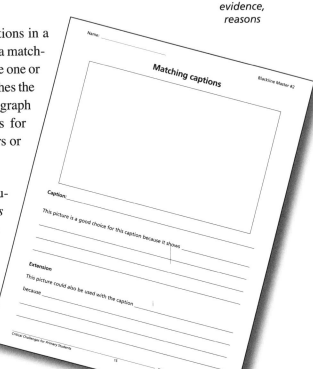

Evaluation — *Blackline Master #3*

Assess the selection of photographs

➤ Assess students' ability to select a good picture to represent the assigned quality using the first criteria on *Assessing photograph selection and interpretation* (Blackline Master #3). The sources of evidence for making this assessment are the students' photographs and/or their responses on *Selecting a good photograph* (Blackline Master #1).

➤ Assess students' ability to match captions with photographs and to provide evidence from a picture to support a choice using the second criteria on *Assessing photograph selection and interpretation* (Blackline Master #3). The sources of evidence for making this assessment are:

• For younger students, use responses from the matching game as they give reasons orally for choosing the picture to match their caption.

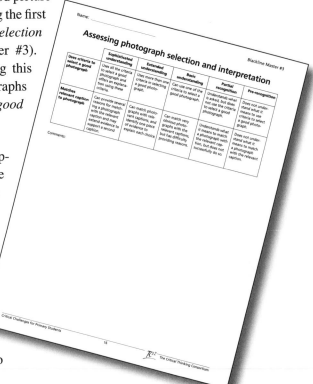

- For older students, use responses on *Matching captions* (Blackline Master #2) to judge their reasons and use of evidence from the picture.

Reaching the "basic understanding" level on the rubric may be appropriate for early primary students.

Extension

Invite reflections

➤ Discuss with the class whether any of the photographs changed how students viewed their community.

Compare pictures

➤ Look for and discuss similarities and differences among the pictures.

Create new captions

➤ Invite students to create new captions for the pictures.

Create a community montage

➤ Invite students to locate and assemble magazine photographs that depict the original captions of the community to create a neighbourhood montage.

Selecting a good photograph

Picture #1   Is it large enough to see?

YES   SO-SO   NO

Do the details help us understand the picture?

YES   SO-SO   NO

Does it match the caption?

YES   SO-SO   NO

Picture #2   Is it large enough to see?

YES   SO-SO   NO

Do the details help us understand the picture?

YES   SO-SO   NO

Does it match the caption?

YES   SO-SO   NO

Picture #3   Is it large enough to see?

YES   SO-SO   NO

Do the details help us understand the picture?

YES   SO-SO   NO

Does it match the caption?

YES   SO-SO   NO

1 ☐
We think picture   2 ☐   is the best picture because
3 ☐

Matching captions

(blank framed box)

Caption: _____

This picture is a good choice for this caption because it shows _____

_____

_____

_____

Extension

This picture could also be used with the caption _____

because _____

_____

_____

Assessing photograph selection and interpretation

	Sophisticated understanding	Extended understanding	Basic understanding	Partial recognition	Pre-recognition
Uses criteria to select a good photograph	Uses all the criteria to select a good photograph and offers an explanation using these criteria.	Uses more than one criteria in selecting a good photograph.	Can use one of the criteria to select a good photograph.	Understands what is asked, but does not use the criteria to select a good photograph.	Does not understand what it means to use criteria to select a good photograph.
Matches relevant caption to photograph	Can provide several reasons for matching a photograph with the relevant caption and may extend evidence to support a second caption.	Can match photographs with relevant captions, and identify one piece of evidence to explain each choice.	Can match very obvious photographs with the relevant captions, but has difficulty providing reasons.	Understands what it means to match a photograph with the relevant caption, but does not successfully do so.	Does not understand what it means to match a photograph with the relevant caption.

Comments:

Design a community

Critical Challenge

Critical tasks
Design a plan for the services and facilities found in an ideal community.

Overview
After extensive study of communities, students brainstorm the qualities to be found in a good community and the services and facilities that best provide for these qualities. Students then design an ideal community using materials of their choice. Students explain how the desired qualities are reflected in the facilities and services in their plan.

Objectives

Broad understanding
Facilities and services available in a community reflect the qualities valued by the community.

Requisite tools

Background knowledge
- knowledge of the facilities and services provided by a city or other community

Criteria for judgment
- criteria for design of an ideal community (e.g., important qualities are promoted, the necessary services and facilities are provided)

Critical thinking vocabulary

Thinking strategies
- T-chart

Habits of mind

Suggested Activities

Build necessary
background experience

Brainstorm
community services

Match services to a
community quality

Extend brainstorm of
community services

Introduce
the challenge

Pre-planning

➤ This critical task is best used at the end of a unit on the village, town or city as a community. It is expected that students have benefited from direct experiences with their own community (e.g., walks around their neighbourhood, tours of shops, visits from local people) and class discussions, books and videos about the idea of city as a community.

Session One

➤ Introduce students to two ideas: (1) the qualities or criteria of a good community and (2) the services or facilities that provide or support these qualities. Suggest, for example, that a good community is one in which the citizens are healthy; in other words, "healthy people" is a quality of a good community. Ask students to suggest some of the services or facilities within a community that contribute to our health (e.g., hospitals, doctors, garbage collection).

➤ On poster paper, create a T-chart using the headings listed below. To illustrate how the chart works, write down the words "healthy people" in the left-hand column and record the facilities and services that students generated in the right-hand column.

T-chart

Qualities of a good community	Services and facilities that support these qualities
• *healthy people*	• *hospitals* • *doctors* • *garbage collection*

➤ As a whole class, have students brainstorm other qualities of a good community and suggest the services and facilities that promote or support these qualities. Depending on the class, you may suggest very sophisticated qualities (e.g., traffic flow, mental health) and "alternative" services and facilities (e.g., solar housing, electric cars). Keep the chart in a prominent place so additional ideas can be added as students progress through the critical challenge.

qualities and services of a good community

Session Two

➤ Suggest to students that they have an opportunity to design their ideal community. Present the critical task:

Design a plan for the services and facilities found in an ideal community.

Students are to identify the important qualities of their ideal community and decide how and in what way these qualities can be realized—i.e., what services and facilities they need in their community.

a good community design

Make a plan

➤ Allow students to decide how they wish to present the design of their community—they may want to consider Lego, big blocks, junk art, drawing, plasticine, and so on. The work may be done in small groups or individually.

Consider the criteria

➤ As students are working on their designs, encourage them to consider the qualities that were generated by the class and to think about how best to provide for the qualities they desire. Encourage students to consult books and other references for ideas on how other communities have provided for essential and desirable services and facilities.

Session Three   *Blackline Masters #1-2*

Present designs

➤ After completing their design, students present them to the class and explain the qualities they have built into their community and what services and facilities support these qualities.

Ask older students to construct a T-chart like the one used earlier to list the qualities of their community and show what services and facilities they choose in their design. You may wish to use the format suggested in *Qualities and services* (Blackline Master #1) or alternatively *Services reflect qualities* (Blackline Master #2).

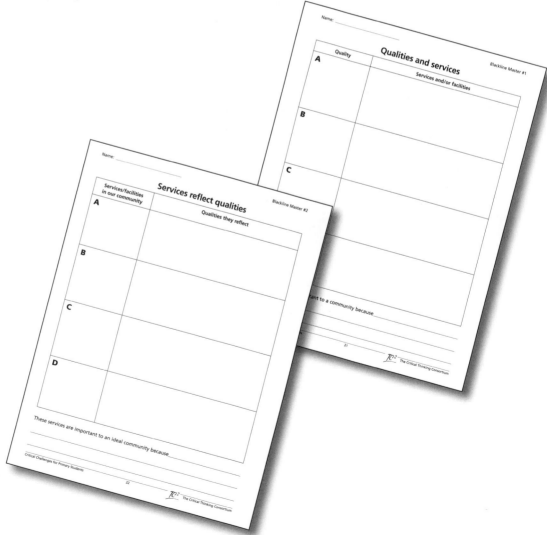

Assess the community designs

➤ Assess students' ability to identify the qualities of a good community, and to design the facilities and services to realize these qualities using the assessment rubric on *Assessing a community design* (Blackline Master #3). The sources of evidence for making this assessment are:

- For younger students, use their construction and oral explanations as they present their community design.

- For older students, use responses on *Services reflect qualities* (Blackline Master #1).

Reaching the "basic understanding" level on the rubric may be appropriate for early primary students.

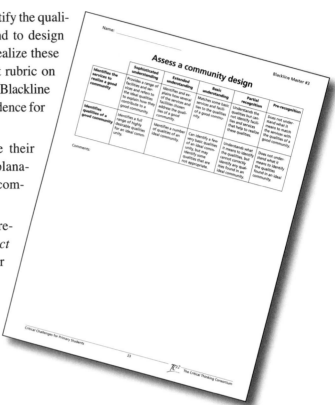

Extension

Peer assess the designs

➤ Invite the class as a whole to assess each design to see which proposals seem to meet the qualities identified by the class.

Join the communities

➤ Invite students to find ways to join their communities together. How would such expansion affect their communities? What new things must they think of? Talk about suburbs, how they are formed and why they occur.

Qualities and services

Quality	Services and/or facilities
A	
B	
C	
D	

These qualities are important to a community because_____

_____

_____

Services reflect qualities

Services/facilities in our community	Qualities they reflect
A	
B	
C	
D	

These services are important to an ideal community because_____

_____

_____

Assess a community design

	Sophisticated understanding	**Extended understanding**	**Basic understanding**	**Partial recognition**	**Pre-recognition**
Identifies the services to realize a good community	Provides a range of facilities and services and refers to the ideal qualities to explain how they contribute to a good community.	Identifies and explains how several of the services and facilities chosen address the qualities of a good community.	Matches some basic services and facilities to the qualities of a good community.	Understands the qualities but cannot identify facilities and services that help to realize these qualities.	Does not understand what it means to match the services with the qualities of a good community.
Identifies qualities of a good community	Identifies a full range of highly desirable qualities for an ideal community.	Identifies a number of qualities of an ideal community.	Can identify a few very basic qualities of an ideal community, but may identify some qualities that are not appropriate.	Understands what it means to identify the qualilties, but cannot correctly identify any qualities found in an ideal community.	Does not understand what it means to identify the qualities found in an ideal community.

Comments:

Insect habitat

Critical Challenge

Critical tasks

A. Think of a question to give us more information about how insects live.

B. Design a desirable habitat for an insect of your choice.

Overview

In this two-part challenge, students observe various insects in the classroom or the natural environment, and study them in films and books. Students work together to identify the features of a desirable insect habitat. Students use these criteria to design a habitat for an insect of their choice. Throughout these activities, students are encouraged to ask informative questions about the life of insects.

Objectives

Broad understanding

A good habitat needs to provide for all of a creature's needs.

Requisite tools

Background knowledge
- habitat needs of various insects

Criteria for judgment
- criteria for an informative question (e.g., is relevant to the topic, finds out something that is not already known)
- features of a good habitat for a particular insect (e.g., safe, near water, access to food)

Critical thinking vocabulary

Thinking strategies
- information webbing
- planning guide

Habits of mind
- inquiring attitude
- attention to detail

 The Critical Thinking Consortium

Suggested Activities

Pre-planning

Assemble student resources

➤ The following books and video, or similar resources that provide information on features of insect habitats, are needed for this challenge:

Video: *In Your Backyard*, David Suzuki

Books: *The Magic School Bus Hops Home*, Patricia Relf, Joanna Cole and Nancy W. Stevenson

The Salamander Room, Anne Mazer

Assemble construction materials

➤ Collect a variety of small construction materials for use in building the habitats (e.g., popsicle sticks, balsa wood, cardboard, paper, string, glue, paper towel tubes).

Session One

Pose questions about insect habitats

➤ Ask students what they know about habitats. Introduce the idea of thinking of questions to find out more about something. Invite every student to think of a question that might help the class learn more about the life of insects. Record all suggestions. Review each question and ask the class to indicate whether or not it is the kind of question that a video on insects might answer. Ask students to listen for answers to their insect-related questions in the video they are about to see. Show the short video *In Your Backyard*, by David Suzuki (or another appropriate resource).

an informative question

needs of various insects

Ater viewing the video, review the student questions to see if any of these were answered in the video. Invite students to think of additional questions about insects.

Create an idea web

➤ In a large group, create a web of the ideas from the video on habitats. Explain that the web is a strategy for recording information, and that students will be asked to expand upon the web as they learn more about habitats.

webbing

Provide additional information

➤ Read *The Magic School Bus Hops Home*. Use this book to add to the web of ideas about the features of a habitat. Invite students to pose additional questions they might have about insects.

inquiring attitude

Session Two

Observe insects

➤ Involve the class in some form of direct observation of insects (e.g., observe how snails grow, study worms in a worm compost, raise butterflies from the larval stage, or go on a nature walk). A strategy for focussing attention while on a nature walk is to place a hoola hoop on the ground in front of a small group of students and have them watch carefully the goings-on for two minutes. After their direct experiences, add to the web of habitat ideas. Invite students to pose any questions that arise about insects.

needs of various insects

attention to detail

➤ Refer to the information web as a means of helping the class develop criteria for a good habitat. Record students' ideas (e.g., supply of water, place to hide, food source) on a class chart.

*features of
a habitat*

Session Three

➤ Read *The Salamander Room* by Anne Mazer, a story about a boy who created a habitat for his salamander. Ask students if they would like to make a home for an insect.

➤ Invite students to think about any additional information they would need in order to build a habitat for an insect. Ask students to work in pairs to consider the following task:

Think of a question to give us more information about how insects live.

Remind students to think of a question about insect life that is not already included in the information gathered by the class and recorded on the information web.

➤ Review each pair's question and collectively try to answer it or decide on a method of finding the answer (e.g., search on Google, check with a local entomologist).

Session Four   *Blackline Master #1*

➤ Present the second critical task to the class:

Design a habitat for an insect of your choice.

planning guide

For younger students, create a chart listing all the things their habitat would need to make it a good home for an insect of their choice.

For older students, provide each student with a copy of *Planning my habitat* (Blackline Master #1) and assist them in recording and finding information and considering the criteria for their habitat as they work on their constructions.

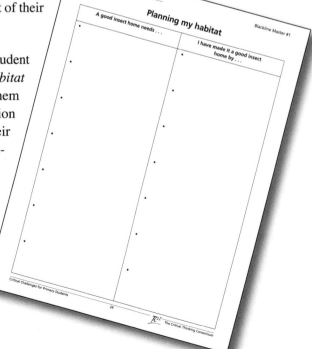

Construct habitats

➤ Provide students with the materials to construct their habitat.

Share habitat designs

➤ After completing their designs, ask students to share and critically discuss each other's designs in light of the criteria.

Evaluation

Assess students' questions

➤ Assess students' abilities to generate questions to learn about insects using the first criterion on the rubric *Assessing the habitat design* (Blackline Master #2).

Share habitat designs

➤ Assess students' abilities to use criteria to guide the construction of an insect habitat using the second criterion on *Assessing the habitat design* (Blackline Master #2). The sources of evidence for making this assessment are:

- For younger students, use their construction and oral explanations as they present their habitat design.

- For older students, use responses on *Planning my habitat* (Blackline Master #1).

Reaching the "basic understanding" level on the rubric may be appropriate for early primary students.

Extension

Discuss the role of habitat builders

➤ As a follow-up, ask students to talk or write about their habitats and their experience in designing the habitats. They could propose ways of keeping those habitats safe and this could lead to a discussion on our environment and how they could help to keep it a safe and healthy place. Discuss what would happen if we were to take away parts of the habitat. How would this change the insect or the environment as a whole?

Build for a class pet

➤ The class may decide to select a few insects as class pets for a short while and actually construct a few of the designs that they thought would best suit their pet insects.

References

In Your Backyard (video) by David Suzuki.

The Salamander Room by Anne Mazer (New York: Alfred A. Knopf, 1991).

The Magic School Bus Hops Home by Patricia Relf, Joanna Cole, and Nancy W. Stevenson (New York: Scholastic Publications, 1991).

Planning my habitat

A good insect home needs . . .	I have made it a good insect home by . . .
•	•
•	•
•	•
•	•
•	•
•	•
•	•

Assessing the habitat design

	Sophisticated understanding	Extended understanding	Basic understanding	Partial recognition	Pre-recognition
Poses questions, seeks information	Probes for information by asking many questions, some subtle and complex.	Poses obvious or simple questions to seek additional information.	Asks questions but not all are helpful or relevant in providing information.	Cannot think of a question they would like to ask about the assigned topic.	Does not understand how to ask a question.
Uses criteria to make habitat design choices	Explains how each criterion for a good habitat is represented in the design.	Links several design features to the criteria for a good habitat.	Can link one or two features of the design to a criterion that are good for a habitat.	Understands what is asked but is not able to link the criteria to a design choice.	Does not understand how to use criteria to design an object.

Comments:

Problem in a picture

Critical Challenge

Critical question

Which of the suggested solutions to the problem situation depicted in the photograph best reflects the qualities of a friendly person?

Overview

Based on a picture card from the *Second Step* series, students explore a situation depicted in a photograph involving a child feeling unwelcome. After brainstorming possible solutions, students select and give reasons for the best solution based on criteria they have generated. Students are encouraged to see that problems can be addressed in several ways but that some solutions are better than others.

Objectives

Broad understanding

Our responses to people who need help should reflect the qualities of a friendly person.

Requisite tools

Background knowledge
- knowledge of ways of helping others

Criteria for judgment
- qualities of a friendly person (e.g., nice to people, is helpful)

Critical thinking vocabulary

Thinking strategies
- information chart
- role play of solutions

Habits of mind
- empathy

Suggested Activities

Make observations about a picture

➤ Select a picture from the *Second Step* series or some other picture set that raises the question of making fellow students feel welcome in a group. Ask students to state what they notice, what feelings the picture brings out and what the picture makes them think of. Encourage students to think how they would feel if they were one of the children in the picture.

empathy

Share solutions

➤ In small groups, ask students to share their responses and discuss possible solutions to the situation in the photograph. Invite each group to share one solution with the entire class. Record these on chart paper.

ways of helping others

Session Two

Establish criteria for friendliness

➤ Ask the class to think of the qualities of a friendly person—for example, doing kind things for people, showing others that you like them, caring about others.

qualities of a friendly person

Share solutions

➤ Set up a chart, such as the one shown below, with three columns. Invite students to brainstorm the qualities of a friendly person and the actions that do and do not exhibit these qualities.

information chart

Recognizing friendly people

Qualities of a friendly person	*Actions that show friendly qualities*	*Actions that do NOT show friendly qualities*
• *showing that you like people*	• *smiles at people*	• *says mean things to people*
•	•	•

Present the challenge

➤ Return to the solutions generated by the class to the problem depicted in the photograph and present the critical question:

> *Which of the suggested solutions to the problem situation depicted in the photograph best reflects the qualities of a friendly person?*

Role-play problem and solution

➤ Ask the students to match the suggested solutions against the qualities in the chart. To help students make up their minds, arrange for different groups to role play the situation in the picture and the varying solutions they have suggested.

role play

Offer an individual response

➤ After discussion anod/or role play of solutions that show the qualities of a friendly person, provide students with a copy of *Picture response* (Blackline Master #1). Invite each student to draw a solution to the problem in the picture. For younger students, ask them to briefly explain the "friendly" qualities and note/scribe them on their drawing. Invite older students to write or draw a response to the picture (or to a situation when they had a similar experience) that they consider to be the most friendly solution to the problem. Ask students to give reasons why their solution is the best by referring to the qualities of friendly people generated by the class.

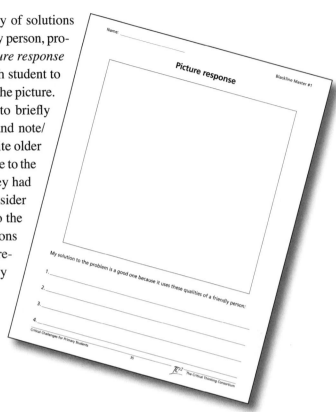

Evaluation

Blackline Master #2

➤ Assess students' abilities to recognize the qualities of a friendly person in their proposed solution using the rubric *Assessing friendly responses* (Blackline Master #2). The sources of evidence for making this assessment are students' explanation of the friendly qualities shown in their solution drawings as recorded on *Picture response* (Blackline Master #1).

Reaching the "basic understanding" level on the rubric may be appropriate for early primary students.

Explore other situations

Extension

➤ Introduce other cards in the *Second Set* series involving the same characters. Ask groups of students to role play various cards. Encourage students to verbalize the problem and a solution.

Reference

Second Step by Kathy Belland (Seattle, WA: Institute for Child Advocacy, 1989).

Picture response

My solution to the problem is a good one because it uses these qualities of a friendly person:

1. _____

2. _____

3. _____

4. _____

Assessing friendly responses

	Sophisticated understanding	Extended understanding	Basic understanding	Partial recognition	Pre-recognition
Recognizes desired qualities in the proposed situation	Identifies obvious and subtle qualities of a friendly person and relates them to their solution to the problem.	Identifies several obvious qualities of a friendly person and can relate them to their solution.	Identifies obvious qualities of a friendly person but may not be able to relate them to their solution.	Understands what is meant but has difficulty identifying even obvious qualities of a friendly person in the proposed solution.	Does not understand what it means to identify the qualities of a friendly person reflected in the proposed solution.

Comments:

The wolf's "real" character

Critical Challenge

Critical question
Is the wolf in *The True Story of the Three Little Pigs* good or bad?

Overview
Students consider a traditional version of the "The Three Little Pigs" and then examine *The True Story of the Three Little Pigs* by Jon Scieszka. In this non-traditional version, the wolf claims to have been unfairly characterized as the bad guy. Students are encouraged to find evidence in the text to support their own conclusion about the wolf's real character. They are asked to see through the obvious rationalization offered by the wolf.

Objectives

Broad understanding
It is important to find and present evidence when deciding on which position to take.

Requisite tools

Background knowledge
- details of *The True Story of the Three Little Pigs*

Criteria for judgment
- criteria for a justified position (e.g., uses evidence from the text to support conclusions)

Critical thinking vocabulary
- evidence

Thinking strategies
- recording evidence

Habits of mind
- open-mindedness

Suggested Activities

Pre-planning

➤ Obtain a copy of a traditional version of "The Three Little Pigs" and *The True Story of the Three Little Pigs* by Jon Scieszka.

Session One

Read first story

➤ Read aloud a traditional version of "The Three Little Pigs."

Gather evidence about the wolf's character

➤ In a large group, record all the events from the text that provide evidence about the wolf's character. If students are unfamiliar with the term 'evidence' ask for a definition (e.g., information that helps us decide what to believe) and provide them with examples (e.g., is helping my parents tidy the house evidence of me being a good worker or bad worker?).

evidence

Session Two   *Blackline Master #1*

Read second story

➤ Read aloud *The True Story of the Three Little Pigs.*

details of the story

Present the critical challenge

➤ Working in groups of three, invite students to consider the critical question:

> *Is the wolf in* The True Story of the Three Little Pigs *good or bad?*

evidence from the text

➤ Ask students to decide as a group whether the wolf in this story is good or bad. Encourage them to identify four pieces of evidence in the text that tell us about the wolf's character and use pictures or words to record this evidence on *Reaching a decision* (Blackline Master #1). Younger students may need assistance in working with a group to record this information on the chart.

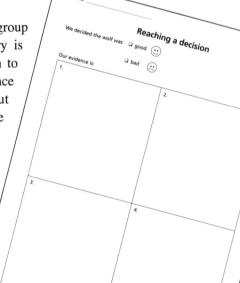

Record evidence

➤ In a large group ask students to share their conclusions and their supporting evidence. As the discussion progresses, use a chart such as the following to record the evidence for and against taking the wolf's version of what happened.

recording evidence

The wolf said or did . . .	Think "Yes" Evidence that supports the wolf's version	Think "No" Evidence that questions the wolf's version

Session Three   *Blackline Master #2*

Re-think conclusion

➤ After sharing the information, invite students to re-think their original conclusion and decide whether or not they want to change their mind. For younger students, designate two areas in the classroom for students to gather. Invite those who did not change their minds as a result of the class discussion to gather in one area, and those students who did change their minds to gather in the other area. Ask "thinkers" from each group to take turns explaining why they have or have not stayed with their original decision. To assist students, provide sentence stems such as:

open-mindedness

- I did not hear a good reason to change and I think the wolf was (good/bad) because . . .

- I did hear a good reason to change. It was . . .

Encourage students to quietly move to the other group if they hear something during this sharing that causes them to change their mind.

Provide older students with a copy of *Re-thinking my decision* (Blackline Master #2) to record their individual conclusions after hearing the class discussion.

Name: _____

Re-thinking my decision
Blackline Master #2

☐ I still agree with my group's decision because

☐ I have changed my mind about my group's decision because

Critical Challenges for Primary Students

42

**Assess ability
to locate evidence**

➤ Assess students' ability to locate evidence from the story using the first criterion found on the rubric *Assessing evidence and conclusions* (Blackline Master #3). The sources of evidence for making this assessment are students' responses to the group discussion and their recorded responses on *Reaching a decision* (Blackline Master #1).

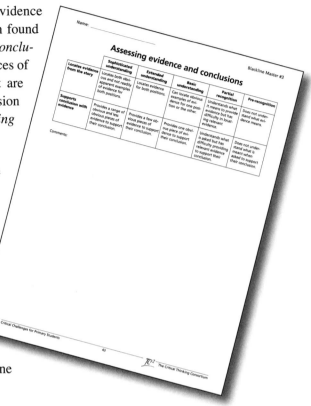

**Assess ability to
support conclusion**

➤ Assess students' ability to provide evidence to support their conclusion using the second criterion found on the rubric *Assessing evidence and conclusions* (Blackline Master #3). The sources of evidence for making this assessment are students' spoken reasons for changing (or not changing) their mind after hearing all the evidence, and students' recorded responses on *Rethinking my decision* (Blackline Master #2).

Reaching the 'basic understanding" level on the rubric may be appropriate for early primary students.

Reference

The True Story of the Three Little Pigs by Jon Scieszka, illustrated by Lane Smith. (New York: Viking, 1989).

Reaching a decision

We decided the wolf was ❑ good 🙂

                                        ❑ bad 🙁

Our evidence is:

1.	2.
3.	4.

Re-thinking my decision

❑ I still agree with my group's decision because _____

_____

_____

_____

_____

_____

_____

_____

❑ I have changed my mind about my group's decision because _____

_____

_____

_____

_____

_____

_____

_____

_____

Assessing evidence and conclusions

	Sophisticated understanding	Extended understanding	Basic understanding	Partial recognition	Pre-recognition
Locates evidence from the story	Locates both obvious and not readily apparent examples of evidence for both positions.	Locates evidence for both positions.	Can locate obvious examples of evidence for one position or the other.	Understands what it means to provide evidence but has difficulty in locating relevant evidence.	Does not understand what evidence means.
Supports conclusion with evidence	Provides a range of obvious and less obvious pieces of evidence to support their conclusion.	Provides a few obvious pieces of evidence to support their conclusion.	Provides one obvious piece of evidence to support their conclusion.	Understands what is asked but has difficulty providing relevant evidence to support their conclusion.	Does not understand what is meant when asked to support their conclusion.

Comments:

Predicting a winner

Critical Challenge

Critical task Use words or pictures to complete Roch Carrier's story, *The Boxing Champion*.

Overview In this challenge, students consider whether or not the author in *The Boxing Champion* by Roch Carrier is likely to win his match. Part-way through the story, students use clues in the text to predict the outcome and justify their predictions. Because the author paints an unrealistic portrait of his prospects, students must infer from the text why he may not win his bout.

Objectives

Broad understanding Sometimes people have unrealistic expectations of what they can achieve in their current condition.

Requisite tools

Background knowledge
- details of Carrier's *The Boxing Champion*

Criteria for judgment
- criteria for a plausible prediction (e.g., fits the story, is more likely or believable)

Critical thinking vocabulary
- evidence or clues

Thinking strategies
- T-chart

Habits of mind
- inquiring or critical attitude
- attention to detail

Suggested Activities

Read first part of story

➤ Read aloud *The Boxing Champion* up to the point where Roch enters the ring after his secret training ("The bell rang. I attacked like a champion.").

details of the story

Look for clues

➤ Ask students to consider whether they think Roch will win the boxing match or not. Discuss the way a detective will look for evidence or clues to suggest what happened or what will happen. Acting as detectives, have students consider clues in the story so far that indicate the outcome of the boxing match and list them on chart paper.

evidence or clues

attention to detail

Create the story ending

➤ Pose the critical task:

Use words or pictures to complete Roch Carrier's story, The Boxing Champion.

Provide each student with a copy of *Win or not* (Blackline Master #1) to complete the story and list the clues supporting their conclusion. Younger students may require assistance in scribing their endings.

Session Two

Gather evidence

➤ Share the different endings created by each student. Use an information recording chart like the one suggested below to record students' evidence from the text indicating why Roch may or may not win the match.

T-chart

Clues that Roch may win	Clues that Roch may not win

criteria for plausible prediction

Discuss the evidence	➤ Ask students to discuss in small groups which outcome is more likely given all the clues. Encourage them to go beyond what Roch says he can do to decide which ending seems more likely.
Share endings	➤ Invite each group to share its decision as to the more likely ending and to indicate two reasons supporting their conclusion.
Read the ending of the story	➤ Read the ending of the story, and discuss why the author led readers to believe that things would happen differently. Ask students to consider any clues in the story that suggest Roch had an unrealistic impression of his boxing talents.

Evaluation   *Blackline Master #2*

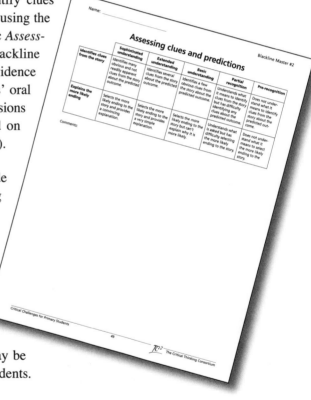

Assess identification of clues

➤ Assess students' ability to identify clues from the beginning of the story using the first criterion found on the rubric *Assessing clues and predictions* (Blackline Master #2). The sources of evidence for this assessment are students' oral responses during the group discussions and writtten responses recorded on *Win or not* (Blackline Master #1).

Assess predictions

➤ Assess students' ability to decide on the more likely story ending using the second criterion found on the rubric *Assessing clues and predictions* (Blackline Master #2). The source of evidence for this assessment is the completion of the story.

Reaching "basic understanding" level on the rubric may be appropriate for early primary students.

Extension

Explore unrealistic expectations

➤ Ask students to share a time when they may have had an unrealistic picture of themselves.

Reference

The Boxing Champion by Roch Carrier, illustrated by Sheldon Cohen, translated by Stella Fischman (Montreal: Tundra Publications, 1991).

Win or not

Roch will   ❑ win   ☺

              ❑ not win   ☹

The story clues I used to decide my ending are:

_____

_____

_____

Assessing clues and predictions

	Sophisticated understanding	Extended understanding	Basic understanding	Partial recognition	Pre-recognition
Identifies clues from the story	Identifies many obvious and not readily apparent clues from the story about the predicted outcome.	Identifies several clues from the story about the predicted outcome.	Identifies a few obvious clues from the story about the predicted outcome.	Understands what it means to identify clues from the story but has difficulty identifying any clues about the predicted outcome.	Does not understand what it means to identify clues from the story about the predicted outcome.
Explains the more likely ending	Selects the more likely ending to the story and provides a convincing explanation.	Selects the more likely ending to the story and provides a very simple explanation.	Selects the more likely ending to the story but can't explain why it is more likely.	Understands what is asked but has difficulty selecting the more likely ending to the story.	Does not understand what it means to select the more likely ending to the story.

Comments:

It's so nice to have a wolf around the house

Critical Challenge

Critical question   Is Cuthbert a hero or a scoundrel?

Overview   In this challenge, students consider whether the wolf, Cuthbert Q. Devine in *It's So Nice to Have a Wolf Around the House,* is a hero or a scoundrel. Students are asked to look for evidence for both conclusions and to be open to the possibility that things may not be as they first appear. After sharing the evidence students have found, they are invited to reconsider their initial conclusion about Cuthbert.

Objectives

Broad understanding   It is wise to consider the reasons both for and against a conclusion before making up one's mind.

Requisite tools

Background knowledge
- details of the story *It's So Nice to Have a Wolf Around the House*
- traits that characterize heroes and scoundrels

Criteria for judgment
- criteria for justified conclusion (e.g., based on evidence, considers reasons for and against)

Critical thinking vocabulary
- evidence
- conclusion

Thinking strategies
- T-chart

Habits of mind
- open-minded

Suggested Activities

Read or view the story

➤ Introduce the book/video, *It's So Nice to Have a Wolf Around the House*. Ask students to pay particular attention to the character, Cuthbert Q. Devine.

details of the story

Introduce the idea of hero/scoundrel

➤ Explain the difference between a hero and a scoundrel. Discuss how heroes and scoundrels act.

traits of heroes/ scoundrels

Present the critical challenge

➤ As a class, ask students to consider the question:

Is Cuthbert a hero or a scoundrel?

Assemble evidence

➤ After a brief discussion, invite students to work in groups of three to brainstorm evidence from the story to support both conclusions—Cuthbert as hero and as scoundrel. If students are unfamiliar with the term "evidence" ask for a definition (e.g., information that helps us decide what to believe) and provide them with examples (e.g., helping my parents tidy the house is evidence of me being a good worker). Using pictures or words, ask students to record their ideas on the T-chart *Collecting evidence* (Blackline Master #1).

evidence

T-chart

Reach a conclusion

➤ Explain that a "conclusion" is the answer reached after all the evidence has been considered. Invite each group to review the evidence and to record a conclusion about Cuthbert on the bottom of *Collecting evidence* (Blackline Master #1).

conclusion

Share evidence with class

➤ Ask each group to share the evidence supporting its conclusion with the rest of the class. Record all the evidence on a large T-chart.

Invite second thoughts

➤ Ask students if anyone wants to change their assessment of Cuthbert's character. Discuss the tendency that some students may have to look at Cuthbert only as a scoundrel because of their feelings about the wolf in Little Red Riding Hood. Inquire whether any students have seen only the good or the bad features of something and later came to see the other side.

open-minded

Record individual conclusions

➤ Provide students with a copy of *Second thoughts* (Blackline Master #2) to record their final conclusion. Encourage students to record the best reasons why Cuthbert might and might not be a hero before explaining the reasons for their personal conclusion. Younger students may require assistance in scribing their thoughts.

criteria for justified conclusion

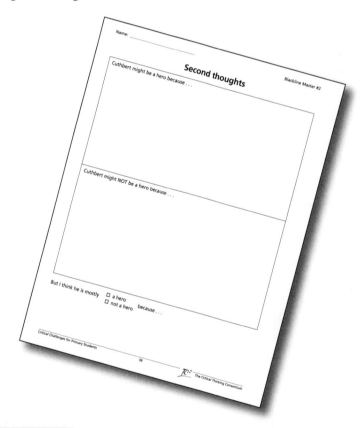

Evaluation
Blackline Master #3

Assess ability to locate evidence

➤ Assess students' ability to locate evidence from the story using the first criterion on *Assessing evidence for and against* (Blackline Master #3). The source of evidence for this assessment is the group responses on *Collecting evidence* (Blackline Master #1).

Assess ability to consider both sides

➤ Assess individual students' ability to consider evidence on both sides of an issue when formulating a conclusion using the second criterion on *Assessing evidence for and against* (Blackline Master #3). The source of evidence for this assessment is the individual responses to *Second thoughts* (Blackline Master #2).

Reaching the 'basic understanding" level on the rubric may be appropriate for early primary students.

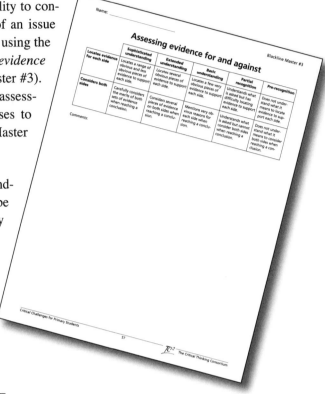

Extension

Consider opposing sides

➤ Encourage students to look at more than one side of things. Ask students to think of a favourite thing (e.g., an event, television program, toy) and find one undesirable feature; and to think of a least favoured thing and find one desirable feature.

References

It's So Nice to Have a Wolf Around the House by Harry Allard, illustrated by James Marshall (Garden City, NY: Doubleday, 1977).

It's So Nice to Have a Wolf Around the House, video produced by Paul Fierlinger, Learning Corporation of America, 1979 (available on YouTube).

Collecting evidence

YES, Cuthbert is a hero	NO, Cuthbert is NOT a hero

Conclusion: We think Cuthbert is_____

_____

_____

_____

Second thoughts

Cuthbert might be a hero because . . .

Cuthbert might NOT be a hero because . . .

But I think he is mostly ☐ a hero   because . . .
☐ not a hero

Assessing evidence for and against

	Sophisticated understanding	Extended understanding	Basic understanding	Partial recognition	Pre-recognition
Locates evidence for each side	Locates a range of obvious and less obvious pieces of evidence to support each side.	Locates several obvious pieces of evidence to support each side.	Locates a few very obvious pieces of evidence to support each side.	Understands what is asked but has difficulty locating evidence to support each side.	Does not understand what it means to locate evidence to support each side.
Considers both sides	Carefully considers the merits of both sets of evidence when reaching a conclusion.	Considers several pieces of evidence on both sides when reaching a conclusion.	Mentions very obvious reasons for each side when reaching a conclusion.	Understands what is asked but cannot consider both sides when reaching a conclusion.	Does not understand what it means to consider both sides when reaching a conclusion.

Comments:

The discovery

Critical Challenge

Critical question　Should Professor Jack share his discovery with the world?

Overview　In the story *Jack and the Meanstalk*, by Brian and Rebecca Wildsmith, Professor Jack discovers a way of dramatically increasing the size of plants. Students brainstorm possible consequences of this discovery and weigh the pros and cons before deciding whether or not Professor Jack's secret should be shared with the rest of the world.

Objectives

Broad understanding　When making a decision, it is wise to consider both the positive and negative effects.

Requisite tools

Background knowledge
- details of *Jack and the Meanstalk*
- applications and consequences of immense plant growth

Criteria for judgment
- criteria for a good decision (e.g., the advantages [pros] are better than the disadvantages [cons])

Critical thinking vocabulary
- pro and con

Thinking strategies
- T-chart

Habits of mind

Suggested Activities

details of
the story

**Read the beginning
of the story**

➤ Read *Jack and the Meanstalk* to the class up to the end of the fifth page beyond the title page. Stop at this point and ask "What are the possible consequences or uses of Professor Jack's discovery?"

**Anticipate
consequences**

In small groups, ask students to use *What might happen?* (Blackline Master #1) to record in words and pictures at least some things that might result from this new way of making plants grow very large.

Session Two

**Introduce
pro and con**

➤ Introduce students to the notion of "pro" and "con" by suggesting that a discovery may have advantages (or desirable outcomes) and may also have disadvantages (or undesirable outcomes). For example, cars help us to get around faster but they also cause pollution. Explain that outcomes that are desirable are called "pro" (promoting or supportive of the idea) and outcomes which are undesirable are called "con" (contrary or against the idea)—"helps us get around" is a pro and "causes pollution" is a con.

pro and con

Identify pros and cons

➤ To check students' understanding of the concepts of "pro" and "con", ask each student to use pictures or word to record two "pros" and two "cons" for attending school. Afterwards, direct students to return to their small groups to consider the four predictions about what might happen if plants grew very large. Ask them to indicate whether their predictions are pro or con by labelling each with a happy or sad face.

Introduce T-chart

➤ Introduce students to a strategy for keeping track of the pros and cons of an idea by presenting on poster paper a T-chart with the heading pros at the top of the left-hand side and cons at the top of the right-hand side. To reinforce the concepts draw a happy and a sad face next to the words.

T-chart

Pro ☺	Con ☹

Share conclusions

➤ Invite each group to present their four ideas about the possible consequences and uses of Professor Jack's discovery and indicate whether each idea should be placed under the pro or the con column. Encourage students to seek advice from the rest of the class if they are unsure whether a consequence is a pro or con. Discuss the possible positive and negative outcomes of each use. For example, an application of Professor Jack's discovery could be to grow lawns. A pro of this application would be fuller, quicker grass; a con would be that it may require a lot more work to keep the lawn trimmed. Invite students to add ideas to the T-chart.

applications and consequences of the discovery

Session Three   *Blackline Master #2*

Present the challenge

➤ When all the consequences (pros and cons) of each application have been recorded, ask students to return to their original groups to consider the critical question:

good decision

> *Should Professor Jack share his discovery with the world?*

Ask students to decide as a group whether the pros—the possible advantages of the discovery—outweigh the cons—the possible disadvantages of the discovery. Ask each group of students to use pictures or words to make a recommendation whether or not Professor Jack should share his discovery with the world. Direct each group to record their decision and reasons on *Our recommendation* (Blackline Master #2).

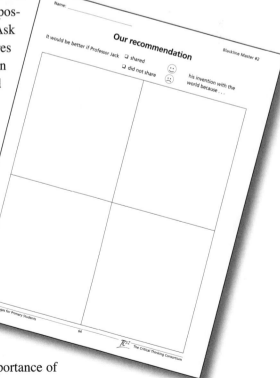

Share recommendations

➤ Invite each group to share its conclusion and to explain the reasoning behind its decision. Ask them to start with the most important reasons first.

Finish the story

➤ Finish reading *Jack and the Meanstalk*. Compare the consequences reported by the authors with the consequences suggested by students. Discuss the importance of considering both the positive and negative effects when making a decision.

Critical Challenges for Primary Students   61   *TC²* The Critical Thinking Consortium

Assess identification of pros and cons

➤ Assess students' ability to identify the outcomes as "pro" or "con" using the first criterion on *Assessing pros and cons* (Blackline Master #3). The sources of evidence for this assessment are the oral responses from students identifying pros and cons for the outcome and the written responses on *What might happen?* (Blackline Master #1).

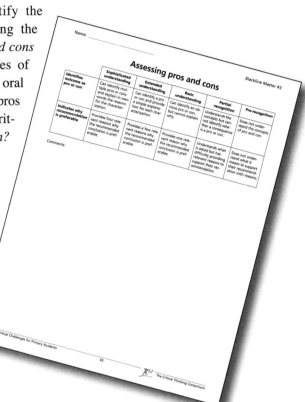

Assess justification of recommendations

➤ Assess students' ability to explain why their recommendations are preferable using the second criterion on *Assessing pros and cons* (Blackline Mastrer #3). The sources of evidence for this assessment are the group responses as they share their recommendations and the written responses on *Our recommendation* (Blackline Master #2).

Reaching the "basic understanding" level on the rubric may be appropriate for early primary students.

Extension

Apply the strategy to other issues

➤ Use this pro and con format for structuring class deliberations around other issues that students are asked to consider.

Reference

Jack and the Meanstalk by Brian and Rebecca Wildsmith (Oxford: Oxford University Press, 1994).

What might happen?

What might happen if plants grew very, very big?

Our recommendation

It would be better if Professor Jack ☐ shared 😊 his invention with the
☐ did not share 🙁 world because . . .

Assessing pros and cons

	Sophisticated understanding	Extended understanding	Basic understanding	Partial recognition	Pre-recognition
Identifies outcome as pro or con	Can identify multiple pros or cons and explain in own words the reasons for the characterization.	Can identify a pro or con and provide a simple explanation for each characterization.	Can identify an obvious pro or con, but cannot explain why.	Understands the concepts but cannot identify whether a consequence is a pro or con.	Does not understand the concepts of pro and con.
Indicates why recommendation is preferable	Provides four relevant reasons why the recommended conclusion is preferable.	Provides a few relevant reasons why the recommended conclusion is preferable.	Provides one relevant reason why the recommended conclusion is preferable.	Understands what is asked but has difficulty providing relevant reasons to support their recommendation.	Does not understand what it means to support their recommendation with reasons.

Comments:

Rumpelstiltskin and the conditions for kindness

Critical Challenge

Critical question
Was it right for Rumpelstiltskin to demand something from the miller's daughter?

Overview
In this challenge, students consider when it is that they have a responsibility to help others in need and when they do not. They view the film *Rumpelstiltskin* and listen to the story before deciding whether Rumpelstiltskin was right to demand something from the miller's daughter in exchange for saving her life.

Objectives

Broad understanding
Sometimes we have a responsibility to help others, and at other times it is largely a matter of personal choice.

Requisite tools

Background knowledge
- knowledge of the story *Rumpelstiltskin*

Criteria for judgment
- criteria for determining responsibility to others (e.g., a person is in need, is part of a promise, doesn't hurt anyone)

Critical thinking vocabulary

Thinking strategies
- T-chart
- story map

Habits of mind
- independent-minded

Suggested Activities

Session One

Examine responsibility to others

➤ Ask students to consider when we have a responsibility to help someone else and when we are free to choose whether or not we will help. Organize the information volunteered using a T-chart such as the one shown below. Invite students to suggest examples that fall within each category.

T-chart

Times when we have a responsibility to help others	Times when we may help others
a person is very thirsty and we have more water than we need	*a person has more than enough water and simply wants more*

Identify criteria for determining responsibility

➤ Based on the examples provided, ask students to summarize criteria for distinguishing when we have a responsibility to help someone (for example, when their personal safety is endangered or when we have promised). List the criteria on a sheet of poster paper: "We have a responsibility to help others when . . ."

criteria for responsibility to others

View the film

➤ Show students the film *Rumpelstiltskin*.

details of the story

Session Two

Create a story map

➤ Invite students to create a story map to retell and internalize the story, and then listen to an oral reading of the story to confirm that they have correctly identified all the main events of the story. (Story maps are geographic diagrams of the events that take place in a story; the focus in this activity is on events that take place in significant locations. Some stories can be more appropriately diagrammed on a timeline; this activity stresses the sequence of significant story events.)

story map

Session Three   *Blackline Master #1*

Present the challenge

➤ Divide students into small groups to discuss the critical question:

Was it right for Rumpelstiltskin to demand something from the miller's daughter?

Remind students of the criteria they identified for deciding when we have a responsibility to help others.

Share decision

➤ Invite each small group of students to present its views and supporting reasons to the whole class. Discuss the issue. During the discussion draw students' attention to the criteria to help them explain why Rumpelstiltskin may or may not have had a responsibility to help the miller's daughter. Provide students with a copy of *Taking a position* (Blackline

Master #1) and ask them to think about the discussion and write down their personal position on Rumpelstiltskin's demand. Encourage students to decide in their own minds what they believe is right.

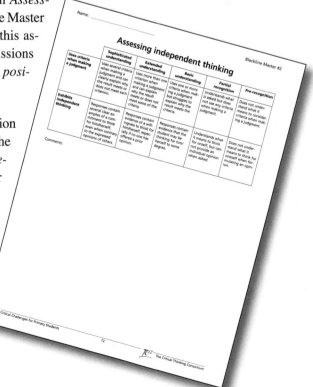

independent-minded

Taking a position   Blackline Master #1

Name: _____

We have a responsibility to help others when _____

Was Rumpelstiltskin ☐ right   ☐ wrong to demand something from the miller's daughter?

I think this because _____

Critical Challenges for Primary Students   71 TC^2 The Critical Thinking Consortium

Evaluation   *Blackline Master #2*

Assess use of criteria

➤ Assess students' use of criteria to justify a position using the first criterion on *Assessing independent thinking* (Blackline Master #2). The sources of evidence for this assessment are the small group discussions and written responses on *Taking a position* (Blackline Master #1).

Assess independent-mindedness

➤ Assess individual student's inclination to think for themselves using the second criterion on *Assessing independent thinking* (Blackline Master #2). The sources of evidence for this assessment are the responses on *Taking a position* (Blackline Master #1) and indications of independent thinking during the class discussion.

Reaching the "basic understanding" level on the rubric may be appropriate for early primary students.

Assessing independent thinking   Blackline Master #2

Name: _____

	Sophisticated understanding	Extended understanding	Basic understanding	Partial recognition	Pre-recognition
Uses criteria when making a judgment	Uses several criteria when making a judgment and can clearly explain why the result meets or does not meet each criterion.	Uses more than one criterion when making a judgment and can explain why the result meets or does not meet some of the criteria.	Uses one or more criteria when making a judgment but struggles to explain why the result meets the criteria.	Understands what is asked but does not use any criteria when making a judgment.	Does not understand what it means to consider criteria when making a judgment.
Exhibits independent thinking	Responses contain several clear examples of a commitment to think for him/herself, even when contrary to the expressed opinions of others.	Responses contain evidence of a willingness to think for him/herself, especially if no one has offered a prior opinion.	Responses contain evidence that the student may be thinking for him/herself to some degree.	Understands what it means to think for oneself, but can not provide an individual opinion when asked.	Does not understand what it means to think for oneself when formulating an opinion.

Comments:

Critical Challenges for Primary Students   72 TC^2 The Critical Thinking Consortium

Extension

➤ As a follow-up, invite students to consider other issues arising from the story:

- Is it ever right to break a promise?
- Was it right for the miller's daughter to break her promise to Rumpelstiltskin?
- Was the King a fair (or good) person?
- Was Rumpelstiltskin any better than the King? (They both demanded material things in return for her life.)

➤ As an extension, present students with critical challenge "L," Right to do wrong?, where they must consider under what conditions it might be permissible to do something "wrong."

References

Rumplestiltskin by Margaret Mayo (London: Orchard Books, 2002).

The Rumplestiltskin Problem by Vivian Vande Velde (New York: Scholastic, 2002).

Taking a position

We have a responsibility to help others when _____

_____

_____

_____

_____

_____

Was Rumpelstiltskin ❑ right to demand something from the miller's daughter?
                      ❑ wrong

I think this because_____

_____

_____

_____

_____

_____

_____

_____

_____

_____

Assessing independent thinking

	Sophisticated understanding	Extended understanding	Basic understanding	Partial recognition	Pre-recognition
Uses criteria when making a judgment	Uses several criteria when making a judgment and can clearly explain why the result meets or does not meet each criterion.	Uses more than one criterion when making a judgment and can explain why the result meets or does not meet some of the criteria.	Uses one or more criteria when making a judgment but struggles to explain why the result meets the criteria.	Understands what is asked but does not use any criteria when making a judgment.	Does not understand what it means to consider criteria when making a judgment.
Exhibits independent thinking	Responses contain several clear examples of a commitment to think for him/herself, even when contrary to the expressed opinions of others.	Responses contain evidence of a willingness to think for him/herself, especially if no one has offered a prior opinion.	Responses contain evidence that the student may be thinking for him/herself to some degree.	Understands what it means to think for onself, but cannot provide an individual opinion when asked.	Does not understand what it means to think for oneself when formulating an opinion.

Comments:

Making a difference

Critical Challenge

Critical question   What might you personally do to make a lasting contribution to someone else's well-being?

Overview   In this challenge, students consider what they can do to make a lasting difference in someone else's life. The inspiration for the challenge is the picture book *A Handful of Seeds*, by Monica Hughes, which tells of a girl in Latin America who helps a group of street kids. Students identify criteria for selecting an action that they might do to make a lasting contribution to others' well-being. They review possible actions in light of these criteria and in groups of three select and explain their proposal for making a difference.

Objectives

Broad understanding   Thoughtful actions can make a lasting difference to people's lives.

Requisite tools

Background knowledge
- knowledge of people's needs and behaviour

Criteria for judgment
- criteria for thoughtful action (e.g., action is meaningful to student, makes a lasting contribution, respects the dignity of the recipient)

Critical thinking vocabulary
- compare and contrast

Thinking strategies
- Venn diagram
- checklist of criteria

Habits of mind
- respectful of feelings of others

Suggested Activities

Read the story

➤ Read aloud *A Handful of Seeds*, by Monica Hughes, a story which tells of a girl in Latin America who helps a group of street kids. Ask for general comments or questions.

Introduce compare and contrast

➤ To develop the notion of compare and contrast, invite students to examine an apple and an orange. Ask them to look closely to see how they are the same as each other (compare) and how they are different from each other (contrast).

compare and contrast

Compare students with Concepcion

➤ Use a Venn diagram (in small groups or as a whole class) to help students compare Concepcion's life and their own. Discuss which of the differences are positive and which are negative.

Venn diagram

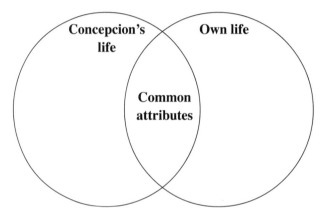

Discuss helping others

➤ Focus on the contribution that Concepcion made and talk about contributions that students have made to other peoples' lives. Discuss why a person might feel ashamed if he or she needed help. Relate this to a sense of dignity. It may be helpful if the class had read *Wingman*, by Daniel Manus Pinkwater, a story about a family that is ashamed to receive a gift of food because the gesture makes them feel poor.

knowledge of needs

respectful of feelings

Session Two   *Blackline Master #1*

Present the challenge

➤ Ask students to consider the critical question:

What might you personally do to make a lasting contribution to someone else's well-being?

Introduce criteria

➤ Invite students to suggest criteria to consider in deciding what they might do to help someone else. If students do not provide them, suggest four criteria for these actions:

- make a lasting contribution to the other person,

- respect the dignity of the recipient,

- be realistic to carry out,

- be personally meaningful to the student.

criteria for thoughtful action

Brainstorm actions

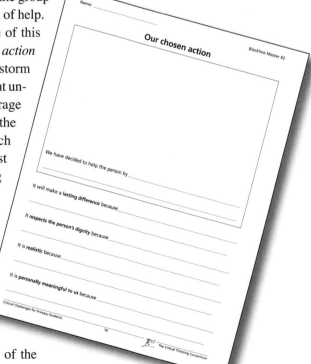

checklist of criteria

➤ Suggest a particular person known to the class who might benefit from some form of help. This could be a person in a story or a recent news report on a local community member. As a class, brainstorm a list of the kinds of actions that could be done to help this person. For each action, consider whether or not it meets each of the criteria. Use a table like *Reviewing each action* (Blackline Master #1) to record how successfully the action meets the agreed-upon criteria.

Session Three   Blackline Masters #1-2

Identify possible actions

➤ Divide students into groups of three to identify a person known to the members of the group who might benefit from some form of help. Invite students to record the name of this person on the top of *Reviewing each action* (Blackline Master #1) and to brainstorm approximately six actions they might undertake to assist this person. Encourage students to draw upon actions on the list generated by the class. Ask each group to match the actions against the agreed-upon criteria for a lasting contribution.

Choose action

➤ Invite each student group to decide on the best action to help the identified person. Provide a copy of *Our chosen action* (Blackline Master #2) for use by each group in drawing or describing the chosen action and explaining why it meets each of the agreed-upon criteria.

| **Consider implementing the action** | ➤ | Encourage students to implement their chosen action, but ensure that students understand that it is entirely up to them whether to do it or not. Ensure that students secure their parents' approval beforehand. Invite each student group to decide on the best action to help the identified person. |

Evaluation

Blackline Master #3

| **Assess use of criteria** | ➤ | Assess students' ability to use the criteria to assess possible actions and recommend an action using the rubric *Assessing lasting contributions* (Blackline Master #3). The source of evidence for this assessment is *Reviewing each action* (Blackline Master #1). |

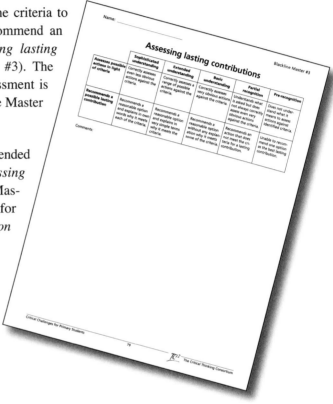

| **Assess recommended action** | ➤ | Assess students' ability to recommended an action using the rubric *Assessing lasting contributions* (Blackline Master #3). The source of evidence for this assessment is *Our chosen action* (Blackline Master #2).

Reaching the "basic understanding" level on the rubric may be appropriate for early primary students. |

Extension

| **Follow-up on the actions** | ➤ | As a follow up, share what students have done—for those who actually implemented their choice: |

- What action did you do?
- How did you feel about your action?
- How did the person feel about your action?
- How could you determine if your contribution has made an impact?

References

A *Handful of Seeds* by Monica Hughes, paintings by Luis Garay (Toronto: Lester Publishers, 1993).

Wingman by Daniel Manus Pinkwater (New York: Dodd Mead, 1975).

Reviewing each action

The person we are thinking of helping is _____

Things we might do to help	Lasting difference?	Respects dignity?	Realistic?	Personally meaningful?
1	✔ X	✔ X	✔ X	✔ X
2	✔ X	✔ X	✔ X	✔ X
3	✔ X	✔ X	✔ X	✔ X
4	✔ X	✔ X	✔ X	✔ X
5	✔ X	✔ X	✔ X	✔ X
6	✔ X	✔ X	✔ X	✔ X

Our chosen action

We have decided to help the person by _____

_____

It will make a **lasting difference** because_____

_____

It **respects the person's dignity** because _____

_____

It is **realistic** because_____

_____

It is **personally meaningful to us** because _____

_____

Assessing lasting contributions

	Sophisticated understanding	Extended understanding	Basic understanding	Partial recognition	Pre-recognition
Assesses possible actions in light of criteria	Correctly assesses even less obvious actions against the criteria.	Correctly assesses a range of possible actions against the criteria.	Correctly assesses very obvious actions against the criteria.	Understands what is asked but does not always correctly assess even very obvious actions against the criteria.	Does not understand what it means to assess actions against identified criteria.
Recommends a possible lasting contribution	Recommends a reasonable option and explains in own words why it meets each of the criteria.	Recommends a reasonable option and explains in very simple terms why it meets the criteria.	Recommends a reasonable option without any explanation why it meets some of the criteria.	Recommends an action that does not meet the criteria for a lasting contribution.	Unable to recommend one option as the best lasting contribution.

Comments:

Right to do wrong?

Critical Challenge

Critical questions

A. Was the father swan justified in stealing the trumpet?

B. Is it ever right to do something wrong?

Overview

In this two-part challenge, the stealing of a trumpet in E.B. White's novel, *The Trumpet of the Swan*, is used to focus discussion on when, if ever, it is justifiable to do something that is wrong. In the story, the parent of a young swan steals a trumpet to provide the young voiceless swan with a way to communicate. Other stories raise a similar dilemma—*Robin Hood* (stealing from the rich to give to the poor) and *Jack and the Beanstalk* (stealing a hen to provide food). Students are asked to offer their preliminary opinions about the acceptability of the swan's action and the appropriateness, in unusual situations, of doing something "wrong." They then explore the impacts of the action on each of the characters in the story before reassessing their initial opinions.

Objectives

Broad understanding

Some actions that are usually wrong to do may in certain situations serve a greater good.

Requisite tools

Background knowledge
- knowledge of the story
- knowledge of the consequences of various actions

Criteria for judgment
- criteria for an acceptable action (e.g., brings more benefit than harm, fair to everyone, done for a good reason)

Critical thinking vocabulary

Thinking strategies
- imagine hypothetical situations
- data chart

Habits of mind

TC^2 The Critical Thinking Consortium

Suggested Activities

Read the story

➤ Read aloud *The Trumpet of the Swan* up to page 80. You may want to substitute another story that raises a similar dilemma—*Robin Hood* (stealing from the rich to give to the poor) and *Jack and the Beanstalk* (stealing a hen to provide food). Invite students to describe what the swan did (i.e., steal the trumpet) and explain the reason (i.e., to help a young voiceless swan). Briefly discuss the first critical question:

knowledge of the story

Was the father swan justified in stealing the trumpet?

Introduce the second critical challenge

➤ In small groups, invite students to discuss the question:

Is it ever right to do something wrong?

Encourage students to draw upon the story and their own experiences to reach an answer. It may be useful to provide a few hypothetical situations to spark students' thinking:

imagine hypothetical situations

• Would it be wrong to steal food from a rich person if my child was starving to death?

• Would it be wrong to steal a chocolate bar from a store owner simply because I wanted to have a snack?

Session Two · *Blackline Master #1*

Reconsider the swan's action

➤ Invite students to think more deeply about the stealing of the trumpet by asking three questions:

criteria for acceptable actions

• Put yourself in the position of the characters in the story who may be affected by the action. Would it be fair to treat them this way?

• What are the effects of this action? Was more good done than harm?

• Was it done for a good reason or simply to satisfy the parent swan's own wishes?

Explore consequences for others

➤ As a class, identify each of the characters who were affected by the swan's action. Re-visit the details of the story, and use a chart such as the following to record on the board how stealing the trumpet affected each character.

data chart

consequences of various actions

How did it affect them?

Who was affected by the action?	How were they affected?

Sort the consequences

➤ As a class, sort the effects on the characters in terms of desirable and undesirable consequences. Record the findings on a chart such as the following.

What good things happened because of the action?	What bad things happened because of the action?

Revisit the first critical challenge

➤ Ask student to use what they have learned about the consequences of the swan's action to reconsider whether the action was justified or not. Provide each student or small group of students with *Thinking about the action* (Blackline Master #1). Explain what is required of them:

- In the top box, students are to indicate and explain whether the action was not fair at all, somewhat fair, or very fair to everyone.

- In the middle box, students are to indicate and explain whether the results were mostly bad, both good and bad, or mostly good.

- In the bottom box, students are to indicate their overall opinion of the swan's actions by checking the appropriate response (no, maybe, yes) and explain their reasons.

Younger students may need help in writing or drawing their responses.

rating scale

Name: _____

Thinking about the action   Blackline Master #1

Is the action fair to everyone?
- ❏ Not fair at all
- ❏ Somewhat fair
- ❏ Very fair to everyone

I think this because . . .

Did more good than bad result from the action?
- ❏ Mostly bad
- ❏ Equally good and bad
- ❏ Mostly good

I think this because . . .

Is the action fair to everyone?
- ❏ No
- ❏ Maybe
- ❏ Yes

I think this because . . .

Critical Challenges for Primary Students

85

Present the second challenge again

➤ Invite students to reconsider their original response to the second question: Is it ever right to do something wrong? Ask them to write their answers and explain why they chose it.

Read the rest of the novel

➤ Finish reading the novel and draw attention to the young swan's efforts to "right the wrong"—to pay back for his father's theft. Discuss whether the swan had a responsibility to try to make up for the wrong.

Evaluation   *Blackline Master #2*

Assess identification of consequences

➤ Assess students' ability to recognize the consequences of an action for various characters in the story using the first criterion on *Assessing consequences* (Blackline Master #2). The sources of evidence for this assessment are students' oral responses when identifying the effects and their explanation for their choices on *Thinking about the action* (Blackline Master #1).

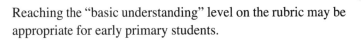

Assess ability to reach a conclusion

➤ Assess students' ability to offer a conclusion that is consistent with the available information using the second criterion on *Assessing consequences* (Blackline Master #2). The source of evidence for this assessment is students' responses on *Thinking about the action* (Blackline Master #1).

Reaching the "basic understanding" level on the rubric may be appropriate for early primary students.

Extension

Consider their own experiences

➤ Invite students to discuss when in their own life they felt that they should make up for a wrong.

Apply to other stories

➤ When discussing another story involving a controversial action, invite students to use the criteria explored in this challenge to assess the acceptability of a character's decision.

Reference

Trumpet of the Swan by E.B. White, illustrated by Edward Froscino (New York: Harper and Row, 1970).

Thinking about the action

Is the action fair to everyone?

      ❑ Not fair at all   ☹

      ❑ Somewhat fair   😐

      ❑ Very fair to everyone   🙂

I think this because . . .

Did more good than bad result from the action?

      ❑ Mostly bad   ☹

      ❑ Equally good and bad   😐

      ❑ Mostly good   🙂

I think this because . . .

Is the action fair to everyone?

      ❑ No   ☹

      ❑ Maybe   😐

      ❑ Yes   🙂

I think this because . . .

Assessing consequences

	Sophisticated understanding	Extended understanding	Basic understanding	Partial recognition	Pre-recognition
Recognizes consequences	Identifies more than one effect of the action for each character.	Identifies an effect of the action for each character.	Identifies a few obvious effects of the action for one or two characters.	Understands what is asked but cannot identify any effects of the action in the present situation.	Does not under-stand what it means to identify the effects of an action.
Offers a consistent conclusion	Selects conclusions that are consistent with the available information and can support each conclusion with more than one reason.	Selects conclusions that are consistent with the available information and can offer a simple reason for each decision.	Selects conclusions that are somewhat consistent with the available informa-tion but has trouble explaining these decisions.	Selects conclusions from the options but they are clearly inconsistent with the available infor-mation.	Is unable to select any conclusions from the options.

Comments:

My character traits

Critical Challenge

Critical task

Identify three positive traits that reflect how others see you.

Overview

In this challenge, students explore the positive features that others in the class would associate with them. Students begin by considering that some people may have an unrealistic picture of themselves. They distinguish character or personality traits that are positive from those that are negative or mixed. Using this knowledge, students choose three positive traits that reflect how others see them. Other students then try to guess which students are described by the identified traits.

Objectives

Broad understanding

We do not always see ourselves as others see us.

Requisite tools

Background knowledge
- personal knowledge of themselves and others
- positive and negative character traits

Criteria for judgment
- criteria for accurate self-perception (e.g., fits the person, reflects how others see the person)

Critical thinking vocabulary
- point of view

Thinking strategies

Habits of mind
- respect for others' views and feelings

Suggested Activities

Discuss unrealistic expectations

➤ Use *The Boxing Champion* by Roch Carrier to introduce the idea that some people may have an unrealistic picture of themselves. It is the story of a boy who believes without good reason that he will win a match with an accomplished boxer. You may want to follow the suggested activities outlined in *Predicting a winner* (Critical Challenge G) to guide students though this story. Ask students to look for clues in the story that suggest Roch had an unrealistic impression of his boxing talents.

Explore personal experiences

➤ Ask students to share a time when they may have had an unrealistic or inaccurate impression of themselves.

Session Two   *Blackline Master #1*

Brainstorm personal traits

➤ Working with a partner, invite students to brainstorm words that describe positive, non-physical, character traits (e.g., funny, friendly, smart). Ask each pair to share its list of traits with another pair. Each group of four is to combine their lists of personal traits. Encourage students to include only those traits that refer to personality or character traits, and not to physical appeareances (e.g., tall, thin, dark hair).

character traits

Assemble master list

➤ Arrange for the groups to share with the class the character traits they have identified. Compile a list of all the words on a large paper or a blackboard. Invite the class to identify any words that do not qualify as personality or character traits.

Sort positive and negative traits

➤ Explain to the class what makes a character word positive. Invite the class to sort the traits into three categories: positive, negative and both. Clarify through discussion where words are placed, especially those in the "both" category. For example, is a word like "goofy" always negative?

Check understanding of positive/negative traits

➤ To check students' understanding of the difference between negative and positive traits, provide students in small groups with cut out copies of the traits listed on *Character traits* (Blackline Master #1). Ask them to sort the characteristics into the three categories.

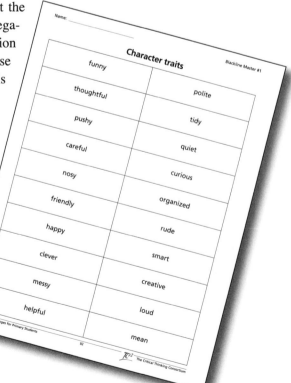

Character traits	Blackline Master #1
funny	
thoughtful	polite
pushy	tidy
careful	quiet
nosy	curious
friendly	organized
happy	rude
clever	smart
messy	creative
helpful	loud
	mean

Introduce point of view

➤ Briefly discuss point of view—how the perceptions of others may not always fit our own perceptions. Remind students of the young boy in *The Boxing Champion*. It may be helpful to physically locate students in different positions (e.g., looking out the window, at the ceiling, at the floor) and ask them to describe what they see from their different physical locations. Ask if students can think of a situation where they saw an event differently from someone else.

point of view

Present the critical challenge

➤ Present the critical task:

Identify three positive traits that reflect how others see you.

Explain that students are to choose three positive character traits that fit how they think others view them. Encourage students to try to see how others in the class might see them. Direct students to record their traits and reasons on *My personal traits* (Blackline Master #2). Invite students to draw a head and shoulders self-portrait in the space provided on this sheet.

knowledge of themselves

accurate self perception

Gather evidence about perceptions

➤ OPTIONAL: Invite older students to gather evidence about their own actions to support their choice of personal traits. Ask students to identify two classmates who would know them and to think of examples from their interactions with each of these students that might support three traits they have selected. Model this with the class by identifying three of your own traits and indicating how students in the class might share these impressions (e.g., I believe Lee would think I was patient because I waited for her to finish her work). Provide students with a copy of *What others think* (Blackline Master #3) to record the names of two classmates and the evidence from these individuals' point of view that might support each trait.

Play a guessing game

➤ Collect the completed copies of *What others think* (Blackline Master #2) and read one trait at a time without disclosing the name of the student. Ask the class to guess which student(s) possess the trait. Invite up to three guesses from the class. Encourage students to explain using examples why they think the word describes the person they identify. After three guesses, invite any students who chose the trait and wish to identify themselves to explain why they believe it describes their character. Remind students not to offer any comments that might hurt anyone's feelings.

respectful of others

Evaluation *Blackline Master #4*

Assess understanding of positive traits

➤ Assess students' understanding of the difference between positive and negative character traits using the first criterion on *Assessing personal traits* (Blackline Master #4). The source of evidence for this assessment is the sorting of the cards found on *Character traits* (Blackline Master #1).

➤ Assess individual students' ability to identify and provide evidence to support their
character traits using the second criterion
on *Assessing personal traits* (Blackline
Master #4). The sources of evidence for
this assessment are the responses on
My personal traits (Blackline Master
#2) and, if used, *What others think*
(Blackline Master #3).

Reaching the "basic understanding" level on the rubric may be
appropriate for early primary
students.

Extension

➤ Secretly distribute to each student a copy of
Another person's traits (Blackline Master #5)
with the name of a class member or a fictional
character they have read about in a story.
Working in a private space, invite students
to draw a picture of and identify three
character traits that describe their secret
person. Afterwards, if students have developed profiles of classmates, arrange
for the completed sheets to be shared
with the person being described. Invite
students individually to compare and
contrast the profile they prepared of
themselves with that prepared by
another student. If students have
developed profiles of fictional
characters, arrange for them to
compare their conclusions with
those of other students who
worked on the same character.

➤ Invite students to think how they might influence other
people's perceptions of them. What could they do to earn additional
positive character traits?

Reference

The Boxing Champion by Roch Carrier, illustrated by Sheldon Cohen,
translated by Stella Fischman (Montreal: Tundra Publications,
1991).

Character traits

funny	polite
thoughtful	tidy
pushy	quiet
careful	curious
nosy	organized
friendly	rude
happy	smart
clever	creative
messy	loud
helpful	mean

My personal traits

I believe I am _____ because _____

_____

I believe I am _____ because _____

_____

I believe I am _____ because _____

_____

What others think

My traits	My friend _____ might think I am like this because _____	My other friend _____ might think I am like this because _____
I think I am: _____		
I think I am: _____		
I think I am: _____		

Assessing personal traits

	Sophisticated understanding	Extended understanding	Basic understanding	Partial recognition	Pre-recognition
Recognizes positive and negative traits	Identifies and explains even subtle positive and negative traits; can see how a trait may possess elements that are both positive and negative.	Identifies and can explain the difference between most positive and negative traits.	Can see the difference between the most glaring positive and negative traits.	Understands what is asked but cannot see the difference between positive and negative traits.	Does not understand what it means to distinguish positive and negative character traits.
Identifies relevant traits	Identifies several traits that show thoughtful understanding of the person and provides good reasons for the choices.	Identifies several traits that pertain to the person and provides very simple reasons for the choices.	Identifies one or two basic traits that pertain to the person but has difficulty providing reasons for the choices.	Understands what is asked but cannot identify any traits that apply to the person.	Does not understand what it means to identify a character trait of an assigned person.

Comments:

Another person's traits

Name of person: _____

I believe _____ is _____ because _____

_____

I believe _____ is _____ because _____

_____

I believe _____ is _____ because _____

_____

Powerful positive memories

Critical Challenge

Critical question Which of your positive memories is your most powerful one?

Overview In this challenge, students are introduced to the concept of memory though the story, *Wilfred Gordon McDonald Partridge* by Mem Fox. This story of an elderly woman who is aided in regaining her lost memory by a little boy is used to stimulate students into thinking about the range of memories they have. After recalling a number of them, students individually select a most powerful positive memory, and explain what makes it so significant.

Objectives

Broad understanding Memories are an important part of our lives and are often associated with powerful feelings.

Requisite tools

Background knowledge
- knowledge of different memories and their qualities

Criteria for judgment
- criteria for a most powerful memory (e.g., vivid, hardest to forget, effect on life)

Critical thinking vocabulary

Thinking strategies
- webbing of ideas

Habits of mind

Suggested Activities

Brainstorm favourite memories

➤ With the whole class, discuss the question, "What are memories?" Invite students to volunteer their favourite memories. Discuss the different features of memories (e.g., good/bad; powerful/faint; reassuring/frightening; funny/sad).

qualities of memories

Read the story

➤ Read the story *Wilfred Gordon McDonald Partridge* by Mem Fox. It describes how a young boy brings things that trigger the memories of an elderly woman who has forgotten much of her past. Review the pictures of the elderly woman's memories. Classify these memories into categories such as happy, sad, funny, scary. Create a web (or chart) on the board to cluster the memories within these categories.

webbing of ideas

Create a web of personal memories

➤ Ask students to work individually to draw pictures or use words to web some of their own memories using the categories introduced above. Reassure students that they don't have to include any memories that are uncomfortable or very private. Encourage students to share their web with a partner. Ask each student who is willing to share one memory with the class as a whole.

knowledge of memories

Confer with parents about memories

➤ Encourage students to take their memory web home and ask their parents or guardians for additional favourite memories to add to their web.

Session Two   *Blackline Master #1*

Present the critical challenge

➤ Ask students to consider the critical question:

Which of your positive memories is your most powerful one?

Offer suggestions about how students might recognize a most powerful memory:

• hardest to forget,

• has had the biggest effect on their life,

• is the most vivid memory they have.

Invite students to add to the list of criteria of their most powerful memory.

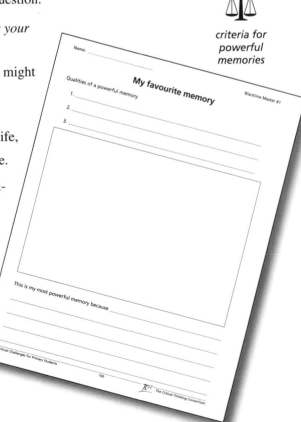

criteria for powerful memories

Choose a most powerful memory

➤ Arrange for students to meet with one or two other students to discuss each student's memories and the reasons they have for seeing one memory as their most powerful one. Ask students individually to use *My favourite memory* (Blackline Master #1) to draw their most powerful memory and explain its significance.

Session Three

Share the memory with the class

➤ Ask students to share their pictures and descriptions of their most powerful memory with the rest of the class.

Evaluation

Blackline Master #2

Assess identification of personal memories

➤ Assess students' ability to recall personal memories using the first criterion on *Assessing powerful memories* (Blackline Master #2). The source of evidence for this assessment is the web of personal memories each student constructs.

Assess choice of powerful memories

➤ Assess students' ability to select and explain their most powerful memory using the second criterion on *Assessing powerful memories* (Blackline Master #2). The source of evidence for this assessment is student responses on *My favourite memory* (Blackline Master #1).

Reaching the "basic understanding" level on the rubric may be appropriate for early primary students.

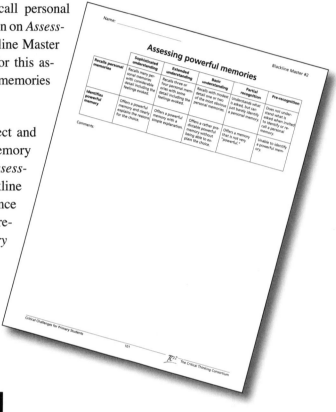

Extension

Write about the memory

➤ Invite students to write about the memory, describing everything they can remember (e.g., the sequence of events, how they felt), and explain why they think it is their most powerful memory. Encourage students to work with a partner, asking each other questions so they can add more detail to their writing.

Explore the significance of memories

➤ As a follow-up, arrange for students to work with a partner to discuss three questions:

- How do memories affect how we act?
- How do memories help us learn new things?
- How can we help ourselves remember important things?

Ask students to write their individual responses to these questions in their learning logs.

Reference

Wilfred Gordon McDonald Partridge by Mem Fox (Harmondsonworth, UK: Puffin Books, 1987).

My favourite memory

Qualities of a powerful memory

1. _____

2. _____

3. _____

This is my most powerful memory because _____

_____

_____

_____

Assessing powerful memories

	Sophisticated understanding	Extended understanding	Basic understanding	Partial recognition	Pre-recognition
Recalls personal memories	Recalls many personal memories with considerable detail including the feelings evoked.	Recalls three or four personal memories with some detail including the feelings evoked.	Recalls with modest detail one or two of the most obvious personal memories.	Understands what is asked, but can just barely identify a personal memory.	Does not understand what is asked when invited to identify or recall a personal memory.
Identifies powerful memory	Offers a powerful memory and clearly explains the reasons for the choice.	Offers a powerful memory with a simple explanation.	Offers a rather predictable powerful memory without being able to explain the choice.	Offers a memory that is not very "powerful."	Unable to identify a powerful memory.

Comments:

Assigning household tasks

Critical Challenge

Critical question

Decide how four household jobs can best be shared by family members.

Overview

In this challenge, students are asked to assign household tasks to members of their family. *Piggybook,* by Anthony Browne, is used to introduce the idea of sharing household chores in a fair manner to the class. Students identify four important tasks in their homes and decide how they might fairly and safely allocate them to family members.

Objectives

Broad understanding

All family members have a role to play in maintaining the home.

Requisite tools

Background knowledge
- knowledge of household tasks
- knowledge of the abilities of family members

Criteria for judgment
- criteria for sharing workload (e.g., fair, safe, able to do)

Critical thinking vocabulary

Thinking strategies

Habits of mind
- fair-mindedness

Suggested Activities

Read the book

➤ Read the story *Piggybook* by Anthony Browne to introduce the class to the idea of sharing household chores in a fair manner. This picture book tells the story of a mother who does all the household jobs, while other family members contribute nothing. After the mother leaves home temporarily, all members learn the need to share in the family responsibilities.

Brainstorm household tasks

➤ As a class, brainstorm various jobs that need to be done to maintain a home. Make a list on large paper or the blackboard of the jobs. Be sure to acknowledge the fact that the tasks will vary depending on the home situation (e.g., whether students live in an apartment or on a farm, whether students are from a small or extended family).

knowledge of household tasks

Session Two

Present the challenge

➤ Present the critical task:

> *Decide how four household jobs could best be shared among family members.*

Explain to students that they are about to decide on four important tasks that need to done in their family and then decide who should do those tasks.

Identify criteria

➤ Inquire about the factors that students might consider when deciding which household jobs should be done by which family member. Help them think about the criteria for assigning household tasks by posing some obviously unsound suggestions such as the following:

criteria for sharing workload

- What is wrong with making one person do everything?
- What might be wrong with asking the youngest member to fix the car?

Guide students to recognize three criteria for allocating household tasks:

- Should be fair to everyone.
- Person is able to do it.
- Is safe for the person to do.

Write the key words (e.g., fair, able to do and safe) on chart paper.

Choose four tasks

➤ Refer students back to the list of household tasks. Ask students to think of tasks that need to be done in their family and choose from the list four tasks that they will assign to members of their family.

knowledge of abilities of family members

Session Three

Allocate tasks among family members

➤ Provide each student with an enlarged (ledger size) copy of *Family jobs* (Blackline Master #1). Ask students to label each box with one of the tasks they have chosen. Using drawings and words, invite students to assign each household job to a family member and illustrate the decisions in the four boxes. Encourage students to consider the criteria when assigning each household job to a family member including him or herself. Ask students to indicate how their decisions reflect the criteria.

Session Four

Present choices to the class

➤ Ask each student to explain their job assignments and give reasons for their choices. Discuss students' choices as a class. Pay particular attention to the fairness of the tasks students assigned themselves.

fair-mindedness

Evaluation

Assess job choices

➤ Assess students' ability to assign jobs based on the agreed-upon criteria using *Assessing job sharing* (Blackline Master #2). The source of evidence is students' responses on *Family jobs* (Blackline Master #1).

Reaching the "basic understanding" level on the rubric may be appropriate for many primary students.

Extension

➤ Discuss different ways that family and household decisions can be made. Who should make the decisions? What are the most fair and effective ways of making decisions in a home?

➤ Discuss the shared responsibilities of different people within a community (e.g., Are firefighters the only people concerned with fire safety?). What are fair and effective ways of sharing duties within a community?

References

Piggybook by Anthony Browne (New York: Alfred A. Knopf, 1986).

Family jobs

Job: _____

Family member: _____

Because: _____

Job: _____

Family member: _____

Because: _____

Job: _____

Family member: _____

Because: _____

Job: _____

Family member: _____

Because: _____

Assessing job sharing

	Sophisticated understanding	Extended understanding	Basic understanding	Partial recognition	Pre-recognition
Judges suitable chores	Judges the suitability of obvious chores for an individual and explains in own words why they are suitable.	Judges suitability of obvious chores for an individual and offers a very simple explanation why they are suitable.	Judges suitability of obvious chores for an individual but cannot explain why they are suitable.	Understands what is asked, but has difficulty correctly judging the suitability of chores for an individual even in very obvious situations.	Does not understand what is asked when invited to judge the suitability of a chore for an individual.
Recognizes the fairness of an assigned chore	Recognizes a fair sharing of chores and explains in own words why they are fair.	Recognizes a fair sharing of chores and offers a very simple explanation for why they are fair.	Recognizes a fair sharing of chores in some cases without explaining why they are fair.	Understands what is being asked, but has difficulty recognizing a fair sharing of chores.	Does not understand what is meant by fair sharing of chores.

Comments:

The trouble with Mama

Critical Challenge

Critical question   Is Monster Mama a good parent?

Overview   In this challenge, students explore the qualities a good parent has. The story, *Monster Mama*, tells of a typical seven-year old whose mother is a Monster. After considering what makes a good parent, students locate four pieces of evidence from the story to help them reach a conclusion about Monster Mama.

Objectives

Broad understanding   People who may not at first seem to be kind may on closer inspection be deserving of appreciation.

Requisite tools

Background knowledge
- knowledge of *Monster Mama*

Criteria for judgment
- criteria of a good parent (e.g., caring, helpful)

Critical thinking vocabulary
- evidence

Thinking strategies

Habits of mind

TC² The Critical Thinking Consortium

Suggested Activities

Brainstorm qualities of a good parent

➤ This challenge may be used on an occasion when students are talking about families or about parents. Invite students to think about the qualities of a good parent. Make a list of their answers. Encourage students to ask their parents what they think makes a good parent and to return the next day with additional suggestions.

criteria of a good parent

Read the story

➤ Read the story *Monster Mama* to the class. Return to the list of criteria of a good parent. Ask students if they wish to change the list as a result of hearing this story.

details of the story

Session Two   *Blackline Master #1*

Identify the most important qualities

➤ Add any additional ideas students bring from their talk with their parents to the list of qualities of a good parent. Work with students to choose three of the most important criteria. This list may include qualities such as caring, fair and helpful.

Present the critical challenge

➤ Invite students to find evidence from the story to answer the critical question:

evidence

Is Monster Mama a good parent?

If students are unfamiliar with the term "evidence" ask for a definition (e.g., information that helps us decide what to believe) and provide them with examples (e.g., helping my parents tidy the house is evidence of me being a good worker).

Collect evidence

➤ Divide the class into small groups. Provide each group with an enlarged copy of *Finding the evidence* (Blackline Master #1) to record their evidence and conclusion about Monster Mama. Referring to the criteria, ask students to draw a picture and write a sentence in each square to illustrate or describe an incident in the story that supports their answer to the question. Each group should agree on the conclusion about Monster Mama's parenting that best reflects the evidence they have provided.

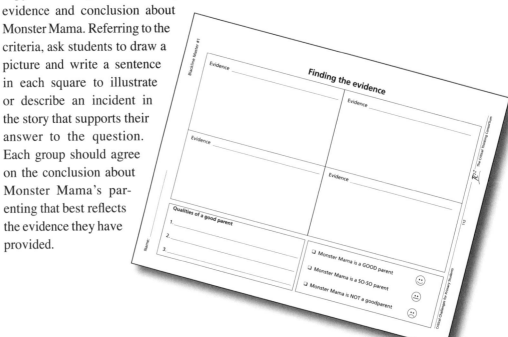

Session Three

Share answers

➤ Invite each group to share its conclusion and the pictures illustrating the supporting evidence. Ask students to indicate which criterion of a good parent is represented in each picture.

Evaluation

Blackline Master #2

Assess supported conclusions

➤ Assess students' ability to identify relevant evidence from the story and to offer a reasonable conclusion using *Assessing the evidence* (Blackline Master #2). The source of evidence for this assessment is students' responses on *Finding the evidence* (Blackline Master #1).

Reaching the "basic understanding" level on the rubric may be appropriate for early primary students.

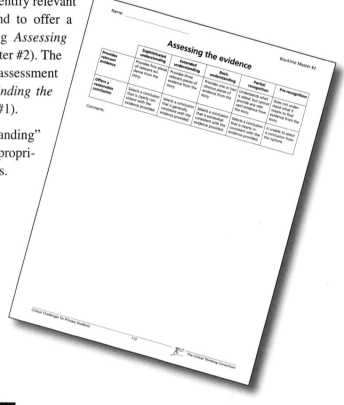

Extension

Apply to other fictional characters

➤ Assist students in refining the criteria of a good parent, and in making use of them to assess other characters in stories that they read.

Reference

Monster Mama by Liz Rosenberg, illustrated by Stephen Gammell (New York: Philomel Books, 1993).

Finding the evidence

Evidence

_____

Evidence

_____

Evidence

_____

Evidence

_____

Qualities of a good parent

1. _____

2. _____

3. _____

☐ Monster Mama is a GOOD parent

☐ Monster Mama is a SO-SO parent

☐ Monster Mama is NOT a goodparent

(: ·) (·: ·) (·: ·)

Assessing the evidence

	Sophisticated understanding	Extended understanding	Basic understanding	Partial recognition	Pre-recognition
Provides relevant evidence	Provides four pieces of relevant evidence from the story.	Provides three relevant pieces of evidence from the story.	Provides one or two obvious pieces of evidence from the story.	Understands what is asked, but cannot provide any relevant evidence from the story.	Does not understand what it means to find evidence from the story.
Offers a reasonable conclusion	Selects a conclusion that is clearly consistent with the evidence provided.	Selects a conclusion that is generally consistent with the evidence provided.	Selects a conclusion that is somewhat consistent with the evidence provided.	Selects a conclusion that is clearly inconsistent with the evidence provided.	Is unable to select a conclusion from the options.

Comments:

Powerful questions

Critical Challenge

Critical challenge   Select a "powerful" question to ask on the chosen topic.

Overview   In preparation for a visit by a classroom guest or written interviews of community members, students identify criteria for a "powerful" question. In groups, students brainstorm possible questions and then use the criteria to critique questions they have generated. Each student selects a powerful question to ask the designated respondent.

Objectives

Broad understanding   Carefully formulated questions can provide valuable and interesting information.

Requisite tools

Background knowledge
- knowledge of the respondent

Criteria for judgment
- criteria for a powerful question (e.g., asks for lots of information, is open-ended, requires thought to answer)

Critical thinking vocabulary
- powerful questions
- criteria

Thinking strategies
- brainstorming

Habits of mind

Suggested Activities

Introduce the idea of a visitor

➤ Explain that students will be seeking information about a topic the class has been studying from a guest who will be coming to the class (or from members in the community). Provide background about the individual(s) and invite students to consider what they would like to learn.

details of the respondents and topic

Introduce the idea of powerful questions

➤ Invite students to consider what would be a really good question—a really powerful question—to ask the guest. Suggest several questions that would likely appear lame or uninteresting to students (e.g., "Do you know what television is?" "Have you ever seen a car?"). Ask students to explain why these are not powerful questions.

powerful questions

Introduce the idea of criteria

➤ If the class has not previously worked with the notion of "criteria," provide a definition (e.g., criteria are how we recognize whether something is what we say it is) and invite students to provide examples of criteria for familiar things (e.g., What does a nice person look like? do? sound like? What would a nasty person look like? do? sound like?).

criteria

Discuss criteria for powerful questions

➤ As a class, identify criteria for powerful questions: "What makes a *powerful* question?" It may help to offer a few samples of powerful and not-so-powerful questions to stimulate students' thinking about the desired qualities. Ask the class to select between three and five criteria that are most important in recognizing a powerful question.

criteria for a powerful question

> ### Sample criteria for powerful questions
>
> - *give you lots of information*
> - *are specific to the person or situation*
> - *are open-ended—can't be answered by yes or no*
> - *may be unexpected*
> - *are usually not easy to answer*
>
> These criteria were generated by a multi-aged class of K-3 students at Charles Dickens Annex in Vancouver, British Columbia.

Brainstorm possible questions

➤ Ask students to work with one or two other students to brainstorm questions they might ask on the assigned topic. Remind students that the purpose of brainstorming is to generate lots of ideas in a short period of time. Encourage students to put aside the criteria for the moment. Stress that students are not to offer any criticism of the suggested questions. Ask students to write out the questions or, if they are not able to do so, ask a friend or the teacher to do it for them. With younger students, you may want to brainstorm possible questions as a class.

brainstorming

➤ Arrange for students to meet with another group to assess each others' questions using the criteria as a guide. Encourage students to identify those questions that seem to be powerful and discuss how they might make the other questions more powerful.

➤ Present the critical task:

Select a "powerful" question to ask on the chosen topic.

Ask each student to pick one powerful question that they would like to ask the guest. Make it clear that students will NOT be required to ask their question if they do not wish to do so.

Questions asked of a World War II veteran

- *Why did you fight in the war?*
- *Do you remember some of your friends from the war?*
- *Which countries did you fight over?*
- *Where did you live during the war?*
- *Were there any women in World War II? If so, what were their jobs?*
- *What started the fighting?*
- *Why was Canada involved?*
- *What was your safe place?*

These questions were generated using the criteria listed above by a multi-aged class of K-3 students at Charles Dickens Annex in Vancouver, British Columbia.

Questions presented in letters to grandparents asking about their school experiences

- *Did your mum or dad ever come to school to help?*
- *What type of punishment did you have?*
- *What was your best friend like?*
- *Can you describe your first day at school?*
- *Can you tell me about your classroom?*
- *What is your favourite memory of school?*
- *How have schools changed since the olden days?*
- *What did you do that was naughty?*
- *We have a really big playground with a climbing pyramid. What was your playground like?*
- *Did you fall in love at school?*

These questions were generated by grade 2 students of Cathy Connolly and Louise Grant at Peak School in Hong Kong.

Ask the questions of the visitor

➤ On the day the visitor comes (or at the time of the interview of community members), invite all students who so wish to ask the question they have prepared.

Evaluation
Blackline Master #1

Assess selection of question

➤ Assess students' ability to select and explain a powerful question using *Assessing powerful questions* (Blackline Master #1). The source of evidence for this assessment is students' final choice of question to pose to the guest.

Reaching the "basic understanding" level on the rubric may be appropriate for early primary students.

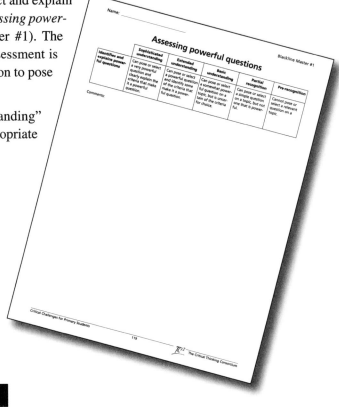

Extension

Revise the criteria

➤ After the guest has left, ask students to consider which questions were the most powerful. Discuss these in light of the criteria generated by the class. Ask if students want to add to or revise their list of criteria that determines what makes a powerful question. Post the revised list in the classroom for future reference.

Apply to other situations

➤ Repeat this activity from time-to-time as other guests visit the class, or when students are framing questions to pursue a topic of study.

Assessing powerful questions

	Sophisticated understanding	Extended understanding	Basic understanding	Partial recognition	Pre-recognition
Identifies and explains powerful questions	Can pose or select a very powerful question and clearly explain the criteria that make it a powerful question.	Can pose or select a powerful question and identify some of the criteria that make it a powerful question.	Can pose or select a somewhat powerful question on a topic, but is uncertain of the criteria for choice.	Can pose or select a simple question on a topic, but not one that is powerful.	Cannot pose or select a relevant question on a topic.

Comments:

The value of money

Critical task
Select the best activity to show what your classmates have learned about money.

Overview
In this challenge, students choose an activity that will enable other students to demonstrate their mastery of a specified outcome involving money. Students examine the curricular learning outcomes related to money, and brainstorm possible activities that would involve one of these outcomes. They then discuss the criteria for a good demonstration task and select an activity that best reflects these criteria.

Objectives

Broad understanding
Students, and not just teachers, can contribute to designing learning activities in the classroom.

Requisite tools

Background knowledge
- knowledge of curricular outcomes related to money
- knowledge of ways to demonstrate learning about money

Criteria for judgment
- criteria for a good demonstration activity (e.g., shows the intended learning, involves all students, is fun to do)

Critical thinking vocabulary

Thinking strategies
- checklist

Habits of mind

Suggested Activities

Teach the concepts

➤ This challenge occurs after students have learned about monetary denominations and have practised the math involved in changing coin amounts. *Alexander, Who Was Rich Last Sunday,* by Judith Viorst, is a good way to introduce this topic.

Session One

Introduce learning outcomes

➤ Share with students the learning outcomes about money in the mathematics curriculum that they have recently explored.

curricular outcomes involving money

Sample learning outcomes involving money

Grade 1

- Identify and describe various coins (i.e., penny, nickel, dime, quarter, $1 coin, $2 coin) using coin manipulatives or drawings, and state their value (e.g., the value of one penny is one cent; the value of a toonie is two dollars);

- Represent money amounts to 20¢ through investigation using coin manipulatives;

Grade 2

- Compose and decompose two-digit numbers in a variety of ways using concrete materials (e.g., . . . compose 37¢ using one quarter, one dime, and two pennies);

- Estimate, count, and represent (using the ¢ symbol) the value of a collection of coins with a maximum value of one dollar;

Grade 3

- Represent and describe the relationships between coins and bills up to $10 (e.g., "There are eight quarters in a toonie and ten dimes in a loonie.");

- Estimate, count, and represent (using the $ symbol) the value of a collection of coins and bills with a maximum value of $10.

Mathematics Grades 1-8 Ministry of Education, Province of Ontario, 2005

Brainstorm possible activities

➤ Form groups of three, and ask students to brainstorm ways of demonstrating that other students had learned one of the outcomes involving money. For example, can students think of activities that would indicate whether other students had learned the value of different coins and could give change for coins? Invite each group to share its ideas. Compile a list of suggested activities for the class to see.

ways to demonstrate learning

Sample activities involving money

- *hold a postcard sale*

- *have a garage sale*

- *hold a cookie sale*

- *collect money to donate to grizzly bear foundation*

- *set up a play store*

- *set up a bank*

- *make up a play about money*

These ideas were generated by a multi-aged class of K-3 students at Charles Dickens Annex in Vancouver, British Columbia.

Session Two   *Blackline Masters #1-2*

Discuss criteria for the activity

➤ Invite the class to discuss criteria for a good way to demonstrate learning about money. Encourage students to think of the qualities that are required to make the experience a success (e.g., shows what they have learned, allows everyone to participate, is fun). Compile a list of their suggestions and invite students to select the three most important criteria that the activity should satisfy. Alternatively, you may want to pick three from this list.

criteria for a good activity

Sample criteria for a good money activity

- *material must be readily available*

- *must have the necessary physical space*

- *all children (ages 5-8) must be able to take part*

- *students must have the necessary skills to take part*

- *must take place during school hours*

These criteria were generated by a multi-aged class of K-3 students at Charles Dickens Annex in Vancouver, British Columbia.

Present the critical challenge

➤ Invite students to consider the following critical task:

Select the best activity to show what your classmates have learned about money.

Divide students into small groups to decide which of the previously suggested activities (or perhaps newly proposed ones) would best meet the identified criteria.

➤ Provide each group with an enlarged copy (ledger size) of one version of *Our choice of activity*. (Use Blackline Master #1 if you want students to consider three pre-identified criteria, and use Blackline Master #2 if you want students to specify the criteria they will consider.) Ask students to draw a picture of their chosen activity and explain how the activity satisfies the three specified criteria (if using Blackline Master #1) or the three criteria that they are to identify (if using Blackline Master #2).

checklist

Session Three

➤ Collect the suggested activities from each group. Ask the class to select (or you may prefer to do this yourself) one or more of the activities that best meet the criteria. With student help, assemble the necessary materials and invite students to take part in the task. Afterwards assess how well the activity(ies) met the identified criteria.

Assess the use of criteria

➤ Assess students' ability to explain how their chosen activity meets the identified criteria using *Assessing the activity selection* (Blackline Master #3). The sources of evidence for this assessment are students' responses on *Our choice of activity* (either Blackline Master #1 or Blackline Master #2).

Reaching the "basic understanding" level on the rubric may be appropriate for early primary students.

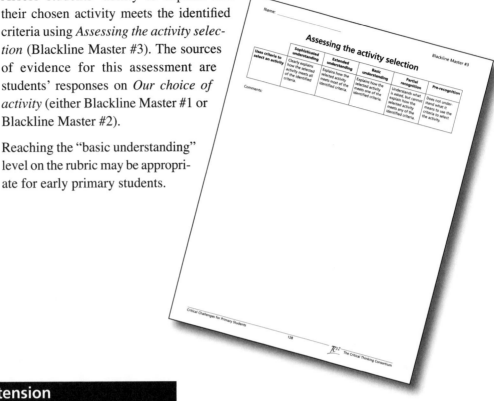

Extension

Apply in other contexts

➤ Ask students to develop activities to demonstrate their learning in other subjects.

References

Alexander, Who Was Rich Last Sunday by Judith Viorst, illustrated by Ray Crey (New York: Atheneum, 1978).

Our choice of activity

Our chosen activity is _____

We think this activity . . .

Criteria		Our reasons
☐ shows what students have learned about money	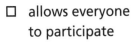	_____ _____
☐ allows everyone to participate		_____ _____
☐ will be fun		_____ _____

Our choice of activity

Our chosen activity is _____

We think this activity . . .

Criteria   **Our reasons**

_____   _____

                     _____

                     _____

_____   _____

                     _____

                     _____

_____   _____

                     _____

                     _____

Assessing the activity selection

	Sophisticated understanding	Extended understanding	Basic understanding	Partial recognition	Pre-recognition
Uses criteria to select an activity	Clearly explains how the selected activity meets all of the identified criteria.	Explains how the selected activity meets most of the identified criteria.	Explains how the selected activity meets one of the identified criteria.	Understands what is asked, but cannot explain how the selected activity meets any of the identified criteria.	Does not understand what it means to use the criteria to select the activity.

Comments: